Advance Praise

"This book shows how to incorporate all of the working pieces for an SOA and provides the reader keen insight on how to leverage these pieces to make a service oriented architecture flourish."

— Jon Richter, SOA Governance Lead, WW SOA delivery team, IBM SWG Services

"[This book summarrizes] the wealth of IBM thinking on service oriented architectures in this concise exposition. I shall be using this in my future SOA engagements."

— Dave Artus, Consulting IT Specialist, WebSphere Services, IBM Hursley Labs

"The first step to consumability is documentation. This book makes SOA approachable and consumable, by providing a big picture view on SOA, and how to take the next steps."

— Roland Barcia, Web 2.0 Enablement and SOA Assets Lead, IBM Software Services for WebSphere

"Exploring IBM SOA Technology & Practice is a comprehensive guide to understanding the anatomy of service oriented architecture, and its corresponding technology. Bobby Woolf's guide will be an invaluable resource for anyone who needs to make technology decisions in order to realize SOA. My team will use it as an educational resource and a quick reference."

— Ben Thurgood, SOA delivery leader, IBM Software Services, Asia Pacfic

Titles of Interest

More IBM Titles of Interest

- *Understanding IBM Workplace Strategy & Products*
- *IBM On Demand Technology Made Simple*
- And many more...

Top e-business Titles

- *101 Ways to Promote Your Web Site*
- *3G Marketing on the Internet*
- *Podcasting for Profit*
- *Protect Your Great Ideas for Free!*
- And many more...

For more information, visit us at *maxpress.com*, e-mail us at info@maxpress.com, or call us in the U.S. at (850) 934-0819.

Exploring IBM SOA Technology & Practice

How to Plan, Build, and Manage a Service Oriented Architecture in the Real World

Bobby Woolf

605 Silverthorn Road
Gulf Breeze, FL 32561
(850) 934-0819
maxpress.com

Publisher: Jim Hoskins
Production Manager: Gina Cooke
Cover Designer: Lauren Smith
Proofreader: Jacquie Wallace
Indexer: Susan Olason
Printer: P.A. Hutchison

This publication is designed to provide accurate and authoritative information in regard to the subject matter covered. It is sold with the understanding that the publisher is not engaged in rendering professional services. If legal, accounting, medical, psychological, or any other expert assistance is required, the services of a competent professional person should be sought. ADAPTED FROM A DECLARATION OF PRINCIPLES OF A JOINT COMMITTEE OF THE AMERICAN BAR ASSOCIATION AND PUBLISHERS.

Copyright © 2008 by Maximum Press.

All rights reserved. Published simultaneously in Canada.

Reproduction or translation of any part of this work beyond that permitted by Section 107 or 108 of the 1976 United States Copyright Act without the permission of the copyright owner is unlawful. Requests for permission or further information should be addressed to the Permissions Department, Maximum Press.

This report was sponsored by IBM. This report utilized information provided by IBM and other companies including publicly available data. This report represents Maximum Press's viewpoint and does not necessarily represent IBM's position on these issues.

Library of Congress Cataloging-in-Publication Data

Woolf, Bobby.
  Exploring IBM SOA technology & practice : how to plan, build, and manage a service oriented architecture in the real world / Bobby Woolf.
      p. cm.
   ISBN 978-0-9773569-4-2 (pbk. : alk. paper)
   1. Web services. 2. Computer network architectures. I. Title. II. Title: Exploring IBM service oriented architecture technology and practice.
   TK5105.88813.W67 2008
   006.7'8--dc22
                                               2007051253

Acknowledgements

The author would like to thank the following people for their help in creating this book: Kyle Miller of IBM Software Group's Worldwide Direct Marketing for conceiving of this book; Jim Hoskins of Maximum Press for recruiting me as an author; IBM technical leaders like Rob High and Eric Herness who created the material this book is based upon; Katie Kean and Geoff Hambrick of IBM Software Services for WebSphere for approving publication of this material; Bruce Clay of IBM IP Law for approving all of the legal stuff; and especially my colleagues at IBM who reviewed lots of drafts and helped make it better: Rachel Reinitz, Kareem Yusuf, Andy Sweet, Guenter Sauter, Matt Perrins, Jon Richter, Dave Artus, Ben Thurgood, Wendy Sent, Roland Barcia, and Owen Cline.

Disclaimer

The purchase of computer software or hardware is an important and costly business decision. While the author and publisher of this book have made reasonable efforts to ensure the accuracy and timeliness of the information contained herein, the author and publisher assume no liability with respect to loss or damage caused or alleged to be caused by reliance on any information contained herein and disclaim any and all warranties, expressed or implied, as to the accuracy or reliability of said information.

This book is not intended to replace the manufacturer's product documentation or personnel in determining the specifications and capabilities of the products mentioned in this book. The manufacturer's product documentation should always be consulted, as the specifications and capabilities of computer hardware and software products are subject to frequent modification. The reader is solely responsible for the choice of computer hardware and software. All configurations and applications of computer hardware and software should be reviewed with the manufacturer's representatives prior to choosing or using any computer hardware and software.

Trademark

The words contained in this text which are believed to be trademarked, service marked, or otherwise to hold proprietary rights have been designated as such by use of initial capitalization. No attempt has been made to designate as trademarked or service marked any words or terms in which proprietary rights might exist. Inclusion, exclusion, or definition of a word or term is not intended to affect, or to express judgment upon, the validity or legal status of any proprietary right which may be claimed for a specific word or term.

About This Book

This book is intended for readers who are already familiar with service oriented architecture (SOA) and who want to learn IBM's specific advice on how to be successful with SOA. It is intended for a wide range of people involved with adopting SOA within an organization: IT executives, business analysts, project managers, architects (application, infrastructure, and integration), and integration and application developers.

This book discusses the following topics:

- How an organization should adopt SOA

- Approaches for discovering and developing services

- IBM's SOA Reference Architecture, a model for the capabilities of an SOA environment

- IBM software products for implementing the SOA Reference Architecture

- Brief guidance on implementing the applications to be deployed into the environment, including the SOA Lifecycle and SOA Governance.

This book will provide you with a good understanding of what IBM suggests you should do to be successful with SOA and how IBM can help.

To learn about SOA in general, a good place to get started is the book *Service Oriented Architecture for Dummies*. For a detailed look at how SOA enables IT and business flexibility, take a look at *The New Language of Business: SOA & Web 2.0* by Sandy Carter, IBM's vice-president of SOA and WebSphere marketing, strategy, and channels.

> **More on the Web**
> - Service Oriented Architecture for Dummies
> - The New Language of Business: SOA & Web 2.0
>
> (soa.maxpress.com)

Your "Members Only" Web Site

The SOA world changes every day. That's why there is a companion Web site associated with this book. On this site you will find the latest news, expanded information, and other resources of interest.

To get into the Web site, go to *soa.maxpress.com*. You will be asked for a password. Type in:

glassy

and you will then be granted access.

Visit the site often and enjoy the updates and resources with our compliments—and thanks again for buying the book. We ask that you not share the user ID and password for this site with anyone else.

Reader Feedback

We welcome your feedback on any aspect of this book, so please e-mail your comments or suggestions to *info@maxpress.com*.

To see our full line of IBM titles, we invite you to visit our Web site, *maxpress.com*. From all of us at Maximum Press, thank you for your interest in our books.

More on the Web

- maxpress.com

(soa.maxpress.com)

Foreword

Today's strong interest in the service oriented architecture (SOA) model for information technology is easy to understand. Information technology (IT), as it has evolved over the last 40 years, has its strengths and weaknesses. At once, IT has enabled great strides in business process efficiencies and has inhibited business flexibility. The more mature the business, the more evident both effects become. So the illusive goal of IT has increasingly focused on keeping the efficiencies afforded by existing IT infrastructure while enabling business processes to be both integrated from start to finish and flexible, enabling rapid change.

Why is business process flexibility so important as to justify a whole new way of structuring enterprise IT architecture? Because flexibility frees a business to respond quickly and in a meaningful way to a changing competitive environment or to go after a new business opportunity that is out of reach of a less flexible competitor. When IT can efficiently adapt as fast as businesses can define new business processes then IT becomes the engine that makes those new ways of doing business a practical reality. That is the promise of SOA.

But have we heard all this before? Some claim there is nothing new in SOA and in some respects this is true. For many years, software developers and architects have been trying to make IT infrastructure more flexible and reusable. And many of the general underlying concepts of SOA have been around in various forms for a long time. But there is indeed something new. The networked world has changed and that change is accelerating. Today's world holds more promise of actually achieving these long sought after goals than ever before due to a confluence of better software technology, widely adopted standards, and a networked world which can leverage the collective efforts of a growing services marketplace. This combination may well lead to a tipping point that enables a whole new level of IT efficiency and flexibility. There is clearly reason for optimism.

While SOA promises greater flexibility and productivity for individual IT departments as they develop and adapt internal applications, its promise is much greater than that. The World Wide Web changed everything by offering a body of information—generated by the collective efforts of the entire planet—to anyone with a connected PC. SOA has the potential to do for services (i.e., software) what the World Wide Web did for information. That is, SOA promises to change everything by offering services—generated by the collective efforts of the entire planet—to anyone developing applications. This is a powerful notion indeed. In fact, emerging marketplaces for SOA services—delivered online—are already appearing and will blur the line between traditional enterprise applications and "software as a service" offerings. Over time, more and more SOA applications will be built using a collection of internally developed services and those offered by third parties over the Internet.

But make no mistake—SOA is not a simple, quick fix, nor is it without risk. SOA requires a complete rethinking of a business's enterprise architecture, processes, and future needs. A business needs to clearly understand the current environment and foreseeable requirements long before any SOA technology offerings are selected and deployed. SOA is not just about taking legacy systems and Web enabling them. In the end, the real benefits of SOA will be reserved for those businesses that can adopt a new way of thinking about IT. With a thoughtful approach, SOA promises to once and for all allow IT to become a better enabler of business flexibility rather than the inhibitor.

As with any period of change, some will choose to sit still and watch the game for awhile to see what happens. After all, there is risk to pursuing an SOA initiative in any organization. But the great promise of SOA means that some will try…perhaps your competitors. So the biggest risk may ultimately be faced by those who choose to do nothing.

Jim Hoskins

Maximum Press

Jim Hoskins is the author of many popular articles and books covering a wide range of technology and Internet business topics. He has been involved with computer technology design, implementation, and education for over 25 years. Jim spent over a decade with IBM designing computer systems and directly helping businesses of all sizes design and implement real-world solutions. He is the author/editor of the popular "Exploring IBM" series, which has sold over 350,000 copies in 12 languages. You can reach Jim via e-mail at jimh@maxpress.com.

Table of Contents

About This Book vi
Your "Members Only" Web Site vi
Reader Feedback vii
Foreword viii

Chapter 1: Getting Started with SOA   1

Adopting SOA 1
   Business Goals of SOA 4
   SOA Considerations 5
   SOA Challenges 8
   Technology Adoption 9
SOA Projects 10
   Project Selection 10
   Project Examples 11
   SOA Center of Excellence 12

Chapter 2: SOA Methodologies   14

Methodologies Overview 14
SOA Entry Points 16
   People 18
   Process 20
      Information 21

Reuse *22*
Connectivity *23*

Chapter 3:
Capabilities of an SOA Application Infrastructure   26

Terminology 26
SOA Reference Architecture 28
Service Providers 29
    Service Connectivity *31*
    Service Support *32*
    Standards Driven *35*

Chapter 4:
Products for an SOA Application Infrastructure   36

Products for the SOA Reference Architecture 36
    Products for SOA Infrastructure *37*
    Products for Human Interaction with SOA *39*
    Products for SOA Business Process Management *39*
    Products for Information as a Service *40*
    Products for Partner Services *40*
    Products for Business Application Services *41*
    Products for SOA Access to Existing Applications *41*
Products for Service Connectivity 42
    Products for SOA Development *43*
    Products for SOA Management *44*
        Service Management 44
        Service Security 44
        Configuration Management 45
    Products for Business Services *45*
WebSphere Process Server Component Model 46
    Process Server Embedded Products *47*
    Process Server Component Model *48*
        SOA Core 49
        Supporting Services 51
        Service Components 53
    Professional Services for SOA Adoption *54*

Chapter 5:
Development of an SOA Application — 56

SOA Lifecycle 56
SOA Lifecycle Phases 58
SOA Governance 60
SOA Governance Challenges 62
SOA Governance Lifecycle 64
SOA Governance and Management Method 65
SOA Governance Products 67

Chapter 6:
Conclusion: Building an SOA Application — 68

About the Author 70

1

Getting Started with SOA

How does an organization get started with SOA? There's a lot to learn, and we need to start somewhere.

Although we have to start with the inevitable question, "What is SOA?" we'll move past that quickly. For readers who want to learn more about what SOA is, there are plenty of books on that; one we suggest is *Service Oriented Architecture for Dummies*. Here, we expand on the standard SOA discussion to add IBM's take on SOA. We focus on the issues and challenges one should consider when adopting SOA, and how to select a good SOA project, and the committee that should manage all SOA projects in an organization.

Adopting SOA

The first question in any SOA conversation tends to be: What is SOA? To quote from IBM's white paper "IBM's SOA Foundation: An Architectural Introduction and Overview": Service oriented architecture (SOA) is "an architectural style for creating an Enterprise IT Architecture that exploits the principles of service orientation to achieve a tighter relationship between the business and the information systems that support the business." SOA leverages service orientation, which is an approach for integrating a business "as a set of linked services." Service orientation enables applications to invoke each other's behavior as services, which can most easily be thought of as "a repeatable task within a business process." A service is self-describing and discoverable, meets specified quality-of-service require-

> **More on the Web**
>
> - IBM's take on SOA
>
> *(soa.maxpress.com)*

> **More on the Web**
>
> - IBM's SOA Foundation: An Architectural Introduction and Overview
>
> (soa.maxpress.com)

ments, and can be managed through governance. Services work together to implement a composite application, which is "a set of related and integrated services that support a business process built on SOA."

The question that may really matter is: Why is SOA important?

Again, quoting "IBM's SOA Foundation": The primary goal of service oriented architecture (SOA) is to align the business world with the world of information technology (IT) in a way that makes both more effective.

SOA focuses on matching IT to the business it helps automate to make the business more innovative. SOA assumes that a business has a business design that "describes how that business works," especially the processes it performs and the organizational structure that performs them. "By deriving the information system design from the business design, an organization can more easily drive changes into the information system at the rate and pace of change in the business design." SOA transforms IT from a cost of doing business to a competitive advantage for rapidly responding to a changing marketplace.

SOA encourages changes both in IT and in the business itself. SOA focuses on developing reusable IT components that automate specific business functionality. And SOA also focuses on designing the business itself as a set of reusable business functions that can be automated in part or completely by IT. New and evolving business offerings should be approached as business processes that can be performed by leveraging existing business capabilities. This makes the new offerings easier to implement for both the business and IT.

Services should make sense both to technical people and to business people. Examples include: get a stock quote, process an insurance claim, change a customer's address, and notify a customer of shipment. Business people should see services as reusable functionality that is frequently used by multiple applications, and potentially by business partners and customers. Technical people see services as application functionality they don't have to implement themselves (or at least have to implement only once), that is available and reusable by any application that needs it, and is an approach to unlock existing assets to derive greater value from them. As business needs change rapidly and new capabilities are developed from existing ones, IT can keep up by quickly building new applications that wire together existing services in new ways.

> **More on the Web**
>
> - Ideas from IBM: SOA for Innovative
> - IMB Systems Journal issue on Service Oriented Architecture
> - IBM developerWorks WebSphere SOA
>
> (soa.maxpress.com)

SOA is the latest evolution of application integration technology... which leads to the question: Why is application integration important?

Modern businesses run on technology. No one IT application can be big enough and complex enough to run even a minimally complex business; a business needs applications for a multitude of functions like order management, customer management, resource management, inventory, and billing. Furthermore, the applications cannot run independently; they need to work together: Order management accepts an order whose fulfillment affects inventory and billing to a customer.

Applications need to be able to work together, and application integration enables them to do so. Whereas previous integration techniques attempted to integrate whole applications, SOA breaks an application into parts-services, enabling a composite application to reuse a part not by embedding the part, but by linking to the part.

SOA is not a new idea, but rather the latest version of evolving practices for encapsulating and integrating application functionality. That evolution is shown in Figure 1.1.

> **More on the Web**
>
> SOA Entry Points
>
> *Webcast*
> *Duration 6 minutes 28 seconds*
> *Registration required*
>
> (soa.maxpress.com)

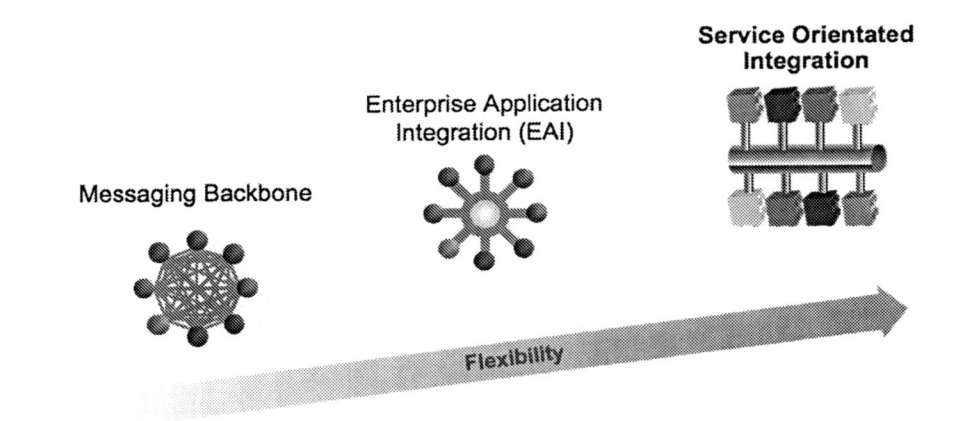

Figure 1.1. Evolution of integration approaches.

Business Goals of SOA

Aligning business and information technology to make both more effective sounds like a good way to go. What goals are organizations adopting SOA trying to accomplish?

Here are some of the business reasons to adopt SOA:

- *Improve B2C communications*—Services used by customers help the business work better with its customers.

- *Improve B2B communications*—Services used by business partners help the business work better with its partners.

- *Create a service oriented architecture for the organization*—A business organized around SOA is more flexible and can respond to business changes more easily and rapidly.

- *Code reuse can reduce development costs*—Services make functionality more reusable, which decreases costs by not having to implement the same functionality repeatedly.

- *Improve integration of existing e-business/CRM/ERP initiatives*—SOA is not an alternative to approaches like e-business on demand, customer relationship management, and enterprise resource planning; it has synergy with these approaches.

- *Provide new revenue opportunities*—SOA helps unlock the value of existing resources and capabilities so that they can be sold and used in new ways.

More on the Web

My CEO thought flexibility & SOA were just IT issues until I told him this...

Webcast
Duration 60 minutes
Registration required

(soa.maxpress.com)

- *Improve internal communications*—Services of one department used by another department help the business better work internally with itself.

- *Address security issues*—Service boundaries provide an opportunity to enforce security aspects, such as managing access and monitoring usage.

- *Improve access to corporate information*—Services can be designed to help make existing corporate knowledge easier to access and can provide a consistent view of "the truth."

- *Create efficiencies across business processes*—Services help factor business processes into reusable tasks so that multiple processes can reuse tasks.

Likewise, these are some of the business benefits of adopting SOA:

- *Functional improvement for end users*—Services can make it easier to provide end users the functionality they want, enable them to access information on demand, integrate people into business processes, and make those capabilities available in a timely manner.

- *Ease of administration*—Services help break large applications into parts that can more easily be monitored and managed, can make the cause of outages easier to diagnose, and can help adequately predict and prepare for future needs. SOA makes monitoring more important but also more effective.

- *Ease of use*—Once services are built, integrating them into new applications is simpler and faster than creating new applications from scratch.

- *Lower IT costs*—Services promote reuse of code and of infrastructure, and simplify administration.

These goals show the enormous potential SOA has to both improve IT and provide business value.

SOA Considerations

Liberating business from technology constraints sounds great. Does this mean all businesses should develop their applications using SOA? Should all applications be SOA?

> **More on the Web**
>
> - Information On demand
> - SOA for People: Accelerate Business
> - SOA Management
>
> *(soa.maxpress.com)*

The answer is: It depends. Most businesses and applications can benefit from SOA, at least under the right circumstances. But not all businesses need SOA, nor are they necessarily ready for SOA. Here are some questions to consider before adopting SOA:

- *Business drivers*—Does the business need SOA? More specifically, does a particular application need SOA? These are some of the considerations that lead a business to decide that it needs SOA:

    - *Accelerate time to market*—Does the business need to develop applications faster and change them faster to quickly meet new business opportunities? If a business doesn't change very rapidly, then maybe its applications don't need to either. Then again, maybe the reason a business historically hasn't changed rapidly is that its IT hasn't been able to keep up.

    - *Reduce costs*—Have IT expenditures eaten up an undue proportion of the business's revenue? What is the return on investment (ROI) for a new application? How long do changes to an existing application take to pay for themselves? Does the business avoid some IT development because it's too expensive?

    - *Increase revenue*—Is the business unable to address opportunities because of inflexible IT? Would better IT enable the business to enter new markets?

    - *Reduce risk and exposure*—Does the business do the same thing several different ways, leading to inconsistencies and errors? How confident is the business that its applications are producing functionality that is correct?

- *Organizational readiness*—Perhaps the business needs SOA, but that doesn't automatically mean it's ready to adopt SOA. An SOA project can easily fail if the organization is not ready for SOA. Some of the prerequisites for SOA success are:

    - *Executive support and sponsorship*—The people who fund projects—and who can take away that funding—don't need to understand in depth what SOA is, but they need to understand how to apply it at a business level and be committed to its success at a technical level. If they're afraid of risk, at the first sign of trouble they'll cancel the project and go back to the old ways.

- – *Skills*—The executives can read a book that convinces them that SOA is the way to go, but that doesn't mean the application development staff knows how to develop SOA applications, nor that the runtime staff knows how to deploy and manage applications. The staff needs training in these new techniques.

- *Current architecture and environments*—SOA can be simpler when developing new applications from scratch, but needed functionality is often buried in existing legacy applications that somehow need to be reused.

  - – *Build and runtime*—SOA applications are built from parts, both during development and at deployment. All the parts have to fit together, not just for one application but for multiple applications, including legacy applications.

  - – *Degree of heterogeneity*—When existing systems have been developed with different technologies and run on different platforms, making them work together is all the more difficult.

- *Operational readiness*—SOA gives applications flexibility, but also adds complexity. More parts means more things that can fail.

  - – *Ability to monitor and manage current operations*—How well does IT currently handle production outages? How easily can problems be diagnosed and repaired?

  - – *Integration of monitoring functions into production environments*—What is the business doing right now? Is more business being performed today than yesterday? Wouldn't this be nice to know?

A business and its IT department should consider these issues to determine whether they're ready to give SOA a try.

More on the Web

- SOA Readiness Assessment

(soa.maxpress.com)

IBM has an SOA Readiness Assessment that can help an organization discover its level of maturity for SOA adoption. The assessment can be run online at the indicated Web link.

SOA Challenges

SOA has many advantages: aligning IT with business, making IT and business more flexible and easier to change quickly, and less lock-in to particular technologies. At the same time, SOA also has some downside. Good IT development techniques become even more important. Here are some specific challenges that SOA can make even more significant:

- *Governance*—Good SOA demands good governance. Who is responsible for developing services? Who prioritizes what to develop or improve next? Who pays for the development, especially when multiple departments benefit?

- *Complexity*—Composing applications of independent and loosely coupled services increases complexity. The more parts there are to an application and the more machines they run on, the more things that can go wrong. When one part of an application fails, it's possible for the entire application to stop working.

- *Reuse*—What do we have and what does it do? Common functionality is often developed repeatedly by teams who are unaware of each other. They may not make their code reusable unless there's incentive to do so. Teams need to know what's available for reuse in order to reuse it.

- *Process*—SOA is a new way of thinking. SOA development is similar to but not the same as traditional object-oriented and procedural development. Teams need to learn new development techniques.

- *Team communication*—Successful SOA brings business and IT closer, but that requires increased communication between two groups that often don't communicate effectively. It also requires that development teams communicate to share reusable assets effectively.

These challenges should not be taken lightly; they have the potential to derail the most well-intentioned SOA project. But met head on, these challenges can be managed to help ensure SOA success.

Technology Adoption

There's a range of approaches an organization can use to adopt any new technology. That range is defined by two extremes:

- *Incremental adoption*—Start small with a new technology and then build. This takes time, but enables teams to learn from their mistakes and build on their success.

- *Big bang*—Covert an application, entire line of business, or the whole IT department to the new technology all at once. This produces results faster, but at far greater risk of failure.

New technology should be adopted incrementally. An organization can have a strategic vision for where it wants to be, but it should start small and incrementally build toward that vision. The relationship between strategic vision and incremental adoption is shown in Figure 1.2.

Incremental adoption helps an organization transform from a starting state to a more desirable one without the transformation being overly jarring or taking unnecessary risk. It helps the organization absorb and digest the transformation, progressing toward greater levels of maturity.

Several well-known practices will help an organization successfully adopt a new technology:

- *Pilot project*—Any new technology should start with a pilot project. A good pilot project should be important enough to get adequate resources and to be useful when successful, but not critical to the organization's short-term goals.

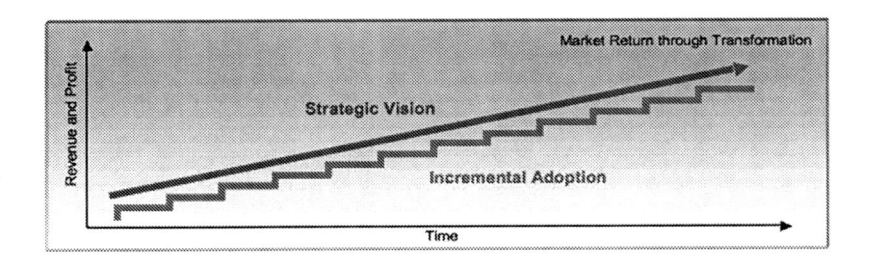

Figure 1.2. Transformation through incremental adoption.

- *Pioneering team*—The pilot project should be staffed with skilled people who work well together and are motivated to be successful with the new technology. They'll benefit if they can get guidance from a Center of Excellence, a team of advisors who have done projects like this before.

- *Lessons learned*—The pilot team should capture lessons learned and use them to quick-start other projects.

- *Incremental development*—Projects should build functionality incrementally, completing some parts before starting others.

These practices will help an organization more successfully adopt any new technology.

SOA Projects

Now that we've talked about the considerations that go into adopting SOA, let's look at what kinds of projects make good SOA projects.

Project Selection

The single most important decision for successfully adopting SOA is selecting a good pilot project. Like any technology adoption, an early SOA project should be important but not critical, should be supported and staffed, and should proceed incrementally.

In addition, an SOA pilot project should:

More on the Web

SOA Demystified! Turn Your SOA Projects Into Lasting Business Success With Higher-Value Services

Webcast
Duration 60 minutes
Registration required

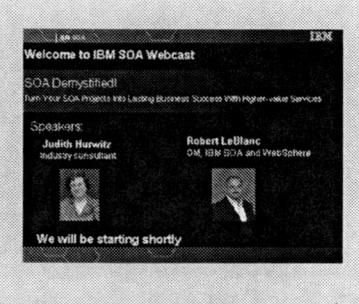

(soa.maxpress.com)

- Address a well-understood business problem

- Incorporate aspects of governance

- Include line-of-business objectives and IT objectives

- Leverage the entry points to SOA

- Require an achievable stretch beyond current capabilities to address gaps (skills, processes, etc.)

- Be something that, if successful, the organization will put into production.

Selecting a pilot project with these criteria will lower risk and increase the odds for project success.

Project Examples

The IBM executive brief "Five SOA Projects That Can Pay For Themselves in Six Months" considers five SOA projects that have been undertaken by real IBM customers. These projects show the advantages of standardizing software around reusable services and the positive impact that has on customers, partners, and the bottom line.

Briefly, the five projects are:

1. *Delivery-date notification service: Providing a single source of information to improve customer service*—This centralized service keeps a major retailer's customers apprised of when an order will be delivered. The retailer estimates this service saves them US$20 million per year in costs; the project costs a small fraction of that.

2. *Transaction dispute service: Automating processes across multiple companies and users*—This project at a financial services organization created an automated process to replace a labor-intensive manual one for resolving disputed transactions. The service produces an estimated cost savings of more than US$200 million per year.

3. *Document verification service: Delivering cost savings through service reuse*—This service for a government agency in the Asia-Pacific region verifies documents such as passports, drivers' licenses, and birth certificates. The

> **More on the Web**
>
> - Five SOA Projects That Can Pay for Themselves in Six Months
>
> (soa.maxpress.com)

    fully automated service replaced a manual one. It was so successful that four other agencies started using it as well.

4. *E-commerce connectivity service: Selling through partner Web sites to increase sales*—This service enables a retailer's business partners to sell its merchandise on their own Web sites. The service provides real-time, controlled access to the retailer's catalog, inventory-management, and order-fulfillment systems.

5. *Criminal justice service: Building an enterprise SOA using CICS systems*—This service for a government agency in North America provides new applications with authorized access to criminal justice information managed by CICS systems. The existing, legacy functionality is able to be reused rather than needing to be reimplemented.

    Thus, a wide range of business functions in a variety of industries can be good candidates to develop into services in an SOA. The trick is to choose one that an organization can use as a good pilot project.

SOA Center of Excellence

Whether an organization is running its first pilot SOA project or has a dozen SOA projects running concurrently, a concern about any SOA project is: Who makes sure that the SOA projects are being run properly?

    IBM recommends establishing an SOA Center of Excellence (COE), a board of knowledgeable SOA practitioners that establishes and supervises policies to help ensure an enterprise's success with SOA. The SOA COE provides thought leadership for how to leverage SOA, is responsible for developing and communicating the organization's vision and strategy for using SOA to meet business goals, and provides mentoring and skills transfer to the SOA projects. The SOA COE not only defines standards, best practices, and policies for how the organization incorporates SOA; it also communicates guidance, monitors and enforces compliance, and evolves the policies. The guidance helps the projects be more successful faster, and the compliance assures the business that the projects are meeting their goals.

The SOA COE is the main tool for applying SOA governance, processes for ensuring that SOA is being used to meet IT and business goals. SOA governance will be covered in a later section. But before we discuss how to govern SOA, we first need to understand SOA and what needs to be governed.

The IBM service offering IBM SOA/Web Services Center of Excellence can help your organization establish its own SOA COE.

> **More on the Web**
>
> - IBM SOA/Web Services Center of Excellence
>   *(soa.maxpress.com)*

2
SOA Methodologies

A methodology is a method, a planned and repeatable process for producing a desired outcome. In software development, a methodology is a set of practices that can be carried out reliably to produce software. SOA, as a new architecture, has new methodologies to help produce applications with that architecture.

Methodologies Overview

IBM has four good methodologies for instituting SOA:

- *SOA Entry Points*—While not a full methodology, this is a simple but effective approach for discovering and developing services. It will be discussed in depth in the later section "SOA Entry Points."

- *Service Integration Maturity Model (SIMM)*—SIMM helps create an incremental transformation roadmap toward higher levels of service integration maturity. It is used to determine which characteristics are desirable to achieve by attaining a new level of maturity. This will determine whether problems encountered at a given level of maturity can be solved by evolving to the next level of service integration maturity. The Open Group is developing the OSIMM standard by merging SIMM from IBM with similar approaches.

- *Service Oriented Modeling Architecture (SOMA)*—SOMA is a method with roles and activities that produce artifacts relating to the identification, specification, and realization of service components and processes. It is aimed at enabling target business processes through the identification, specification, and realization of business-aligned services that form the SOA foundation. It creates continuity between the business intent and IT implementation by extending business characteristics (e.g., goals and key performance indicators) into the IT analysis and architectural decisions. Analysis and modeling performed during SOMA are technology and product agnostic, but establish a context for making technology—and product—specific decisions in later phases of the lifecycle. Its goal is to provide guidance in the modeling (analysis and design) of SOA. There is a SOMA plug-in for the Rational Unified Process (RUP).

- *Component Business Modeling (CBM)*—CBM is a method whereby organizations can identify opportunities for improvement and innovation. The model regroups the organization's activities into a manageable number of discrete, modular, and reusable components. These business components enable flexibility and provide for a clarified focus on the core capabilities needed to run the business and drive business strategy. CBM helps an organization determine where to focus business innovation in order to derive maximum benefit. When that innovation can be realized as SOA applications, then CBM helps to ensure that SOA provides maximum strategic value to the organization.

These methodologies are listed in order of scope. The entry points focus on identifying and developing individual services. SIMM takes existing services and considers how to improve them. SOMA is a technique to apply SOA to an entire application, department, or enterprise. CBM goes beyond software and models the business itself as a set of reusable components. The earlier techniques are simpler for getting started. These latter techniques require a more coordinated effort over a longer period of time, but can more quickly produce a much more radical transformation of an organization.

There is also a methodology for governance:

- *SOA Governance and Management Method (SGMM)*—SGMM helps an organization develop a strategy for SOA governance. It is described in more detail in the later section "SOA Governance and Management Method."

These methodologies are very extensive and could require a whole book to document completely, which is much more space than we have here. Please see the links for sources of additional information.

> **More on the Web**
>
> - Increase Flexibility with the Service Integration Maturity Model
> - IBM Service Oriented Modeling Architecture (White Paper)
> - IBM Service Oriented Modeling Architecture (Article)
> - SOMA plug-in for the Rational Unified Process
> - Component Business Modeling
> - The Open Group Service Integration Security Model
>
> *(soa.maxpress.com)*

SOA Entry Points

Earlier in "Methodologies Overview" we mentioned the SOA entry points (one of the ideas from IBM), a simple approach to get started discovering and developing services a few at a time. In this section, we explore what the entry points are and why they're helpful for developing SOA applications.

The IBM white paper "Entry Points into SOA: Taking a Business-centric Approach" describes five specific approaches for getting started with SOA. The SOA entry points are distinct and consumable starting points requiring a limited set of products and skills to get started.

Three of the SOA entry points are business-centric, applying directly to the tasks businesses perform to produce value for customers. These business-centric entry points are:

- *People*—Productivity through people collaboration

- *Process*—Business process management for continuous innovation

- *Information*—Delivering information as a service.

> **More on the Web**
>
> How to Integrate People and Processes with SOA
>
> *Webcast*
> *Duration 60 minutes*
> *Registration required*
>
> *(soa.maxpress.com)*

SOA Methodologies **17**

The remaining two SOA entry points are IT-centric. They are not as immediately recognizable by business people, but they help to integrate and reuse the business-centric SOA services. They are also technology-focused approaches IT can use to get started with SOA. These IT-centric entry points are:

> **More on the Web**
>
> - SOA Entry Points
> - Ideas from IBM: SOA Entry Points
> - Entry points Into SOA: Taking a Business-Centric Approach
>
> *(soa.maxpress.com)*

- *Reuse*—Creating reusable functionality

- *Connectivity*—Underlying connectivity to support business-centric SOA.

The relationship among the five SOA entry points can be envisioned as shown in Figure 2.1. Figure 2.2 gives an overview of what the entry points are and the value they provide companies.

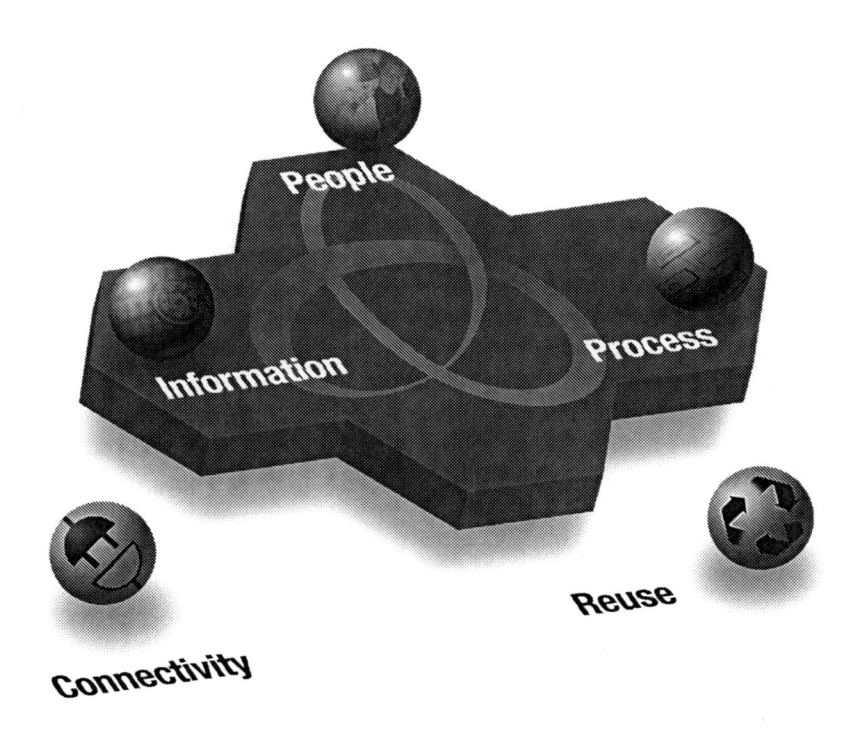

Figure 2.1. Five entry points into SOA.

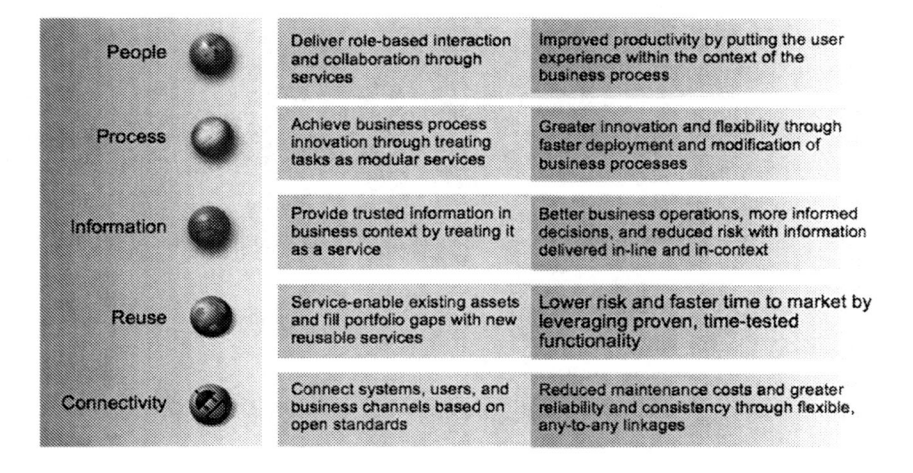

People	Deliver role-based interaction and collaboration through services	Improved productivity by putting the user experience within the context of the business process
Process	Achieve business process innovation through treating tasks as modular services	Greater innovation and flexibility through faster deployment and modification of business processes
Information	Provide trusted information in business context by treating it as a service	Better business operations, more informed decisions, and reduced risk with information delivered in-line and in-context
Reuse	Service-enable existing assets and fill portfolio gaps with new reusable services	Lower risk and faster time to market by leveraging proven, time-tested functionality
Connectivity	Connect systems, users, and business channels based on open standards	Reduced maintenance costs and greater reliability and consistency through flexible, any-to-any linkages

Figure 2.2. SOA entry points and their value to companies.

The entry points are distinct but can be used in combination. They are techniques to use to discover what services are needed and to develop those services. They're ways to look at the requirements for applications and business capabilities and figure out what services are needed.

Let's explore the entry points in detail.

People

The people entry point focuses on services that enable human users—employees, partners, and customers—to be more productive and to collaborate more effectively. Such services can aggregate information from otherwise unrelated sources based on each user's specific context. They can interact with business processes to enable humans to participate in otherwise automated and centrally managed processes. These user-oriented services hide the boundaries created by separate applications and data centers, presenting a unified experience that is exactly what the user needs.

People-focused services unite user interfaces and SOA. They provide users with the interfaces they need to perform their tasks, even if the systems that perform the work don't really work that way. User interfaces composed of services break the interface into task-based parts which can be reused whenever a user needs to perform that task, such as on separate screens, and by different users that need to perform the same task, even in different contexts. They make user interfaces modular and reusable.

People-focused services can be implemented using any technology for user interface components, typically a graphical user interface (GUI). GUIs today are often Web interfaces created from dynamically generated HTML, produced by technologies like JavaServer Pages (JSP), portlets, and Asynchronous JavaScript and XML (Ajax). A JSP can accept input used to invoke a service and can display the service's output. A portlet is a reusable GUI segment designed to be composed with others in a single portal screen. A service portlet accesses its data from a service and then displays it in the portal; the configuration of the portlet often acts as input to the service. New portal screens can easily be built by combining together existing portlets, each of which just needs its corresponding service to be available at runtime. Likewise, people-focused services can be used to support Web 2.0 GUIs, such as the Ajax technique for interactive Web GUIs, which retrieves new data for a display by asynchronously invoking a service. People-focused services can also be used to develop alternative user I/O, such as GUIs for the limited screens on mobile devices and audio I/O for telephone access.

> **More on the Web**
>
> - Innovations at the Front End of SOA
>   (soa.maxpress.com)

The value of people-focused services is that they enable users to exploit services and even act as services, and to experience the benefits of SOA directly. Composite applications, especially those with portal and/or Web 2.0 GUIs, can be created, deployed, and updated easier, faster, and more reliably using SOA techniques.

People-focused services fit well into SOA because they enable the user interface to be composed of services. A composite application can be custom-composed of reusable services, and then its UI can likewise be custom-created using widgets that already know how to display and interact with those services. Because this unified model is a set of services, it can be reused for different types of users, creating consistency of user experience and eliminating redundant efforts to implement these experiences.

There are a couple of good ways to get started developing people services. Look for business tasks people perform that require them to access several separate applications. Also look for tasks requiring lots of different information, or tasks where the information needed differs for different types of users in different contexts. Services like these can be extended to create alert-driven dashboards that let people know when there is work to be performed.

Process

The process entry point focuses on services that enable businesses to automate their business processes—a predictable chain of tasks that produces a business result. An organization uses this entry point to build business processes from reusable components, optimize them, and then easily update them and monitor their execution.

Process services unite workflow and SOA. They enable an enterprise to identify its business's workflows—predictable and repeatable efforts that are performed in a coordinated series of steps by various people or machines in understood roles—and make them into services. Capturing the steps in the workflow helps with understanding how to automate those steps; when all of the steps can be automated, the entire workflow is automated. These services help identify the know-how people have in their heads for how work gets done and capture it in computer software where it can be used to coordinate activities in a much more controlled, traceable, and scalable manner.

Process services are often implemented using business process execution language (BPEL), an XML document schema for describing business processes. Systems analysts and developers use business process editors to develop business processes, whose output is BPEL. Administrators then deploy the BPEL into a business process engine that executes the business process at runtime. The current BPEL standard does not support human interaction, and so is often supplemented with other emerging standards like WS-BPEL Extension for People.

A value of process-focused services is that they enable systems analysts to quickly and easily describe what a business should do without initially getting bogged down in the details of how it should do it. For example, processing an insurance claim can look as simple as: gather details, verify details, adjust claim, and issue payment. Those steps can be implemented separately; the way a particular step works may be completely redesigned, but the overall process remains valid. The process is not lost in the code, but is externalized where it can easily be understood, measured, and adjusted.

Process services fit well into SOA because the process itself is a service and each activity in the process is a service. New services can be created easily by developing new processes that combine existing services together in new ways. Business processes lend themselves to monitoring, with their status displayed in dashboards.

To start developing a process service, look for a business process that needs better automation or monitoring. Such processes often run as batches in the background: A customer submits an order, a policy holder submits a claim, and a business partner makes a change affecting several systems. A business process can start immediately, and automatically creates a history of how many are running and what they're doing. The services used to develop a business process can then be reused in different compositions to develop other business processes.

Information

The information entry point focuses on services that enable all applications to access and update the same consistent view of data, as if the entire enterprise contained just a single database. Traditionally, each application implements its own data access to what is supposed to be the same data. Data spread across multiple databases and inconsistencies in data access can lead to different applications answering the same query differently, causing inconsistent user experiences. Likewise, the same information must sometimes be stored in multiple databases, which means that each application that updates the data must update all of the databases consistently. When the data is moved or the format must be changed, each application using the data must be independently updated, which can cause more inconsistencies.

Information as a service unites information management and SOA. These services deliver accurate, timely, integrated information in the right context as a service. Multiple applications can reuse the same information services, which simplifies the applications, enhances consistency, and avoids redundancy. Encapsulating access to highly reusable data leads to highly reusable information services. Many applications need access to the databases of records that contain the enterprise's master data, like customers, products, and accounts. Information services not only provide consistent, reusable access to this data, but because it is often distributed across multiple databases, the services integrate the data and provide a single consistent view of "the truth."

Information services can best be implemented using a data integrator that acts like a database with a services interface but is capable of performing extensive processing on the data. The simplest services provide reusable access to CRUD—create, read, update, and delete—the data, both structured and unstructured. More powerful services integrate information that resides in a range of heterogeneous repositories, possibly with redundant and inconsistent information—data that may need to be cleansed, consolidated, and/or enriched. Services also simplify access to external sources of data, such as querying a business partner's inventory.

The value of information-focused services is that they hide the details of how the data is accessed. As new sources are added, old ones removed, and data rearranged, only the service implementations need to be updated; the applications using the services remain unaffected.

Information services fit well into SOA because they enable an SOA application to treat information as a service. Services typically perform business functionality, but sometimes that functionality is essentially to CRUD some data. A business process to fulfill a purchase order may need to access a customer's credit profile; that access can be a service that simply retrieves the profile data. That profile data may be scattered among different databases needing integration, and may need enrichment and cleansing. Those databases may be different tomorrow than they are today; in all cases, the service hides those details. The process may also need to update the purchase order. It can do so using a service that hides what databases and schemas are actually used to store the order.

To start developing an information service, look for data that needs to be accessed—read and/or written—by a variety of applications, especially data that needs to be made available to business partners in a controlled fashion. A key example

> **More on the Web**
>
> Master Data Management with SOA:
> Enabling Rich Interaction
>
> *Webcast*
> *Duration 50 minutes 15 seconds*
> *Registration required*
>
> *(soa.maxpress.com)*

would be access to databases of record for master data elements. This approach is especially helpful when the applications do not agree entirely on the data format to be used, when the data is partitioned or duplicated across multiple databases, or when the data needs to be cleansed. The service provides a single point of access for all applications that need to read and/or write the data. Information services then lead themselves to monitoring to determine if and when specific data is being used.

Reuse

The reuse entry point focuses on services that enable applications to share functionality. A reusable service provides reuse not just at development time, through shared code, but at runtime, through a shared execution environment. It is an especially good approach to access existing functionality in so-called legacy systems. A reusable service may or may not map nicely to an easily recognized business task; it may be an IT service that nicely encapsulates behavior that several applications need.

A reusable service unites code reuse and SOA. Reusable code and components have been a key goal of software development; service orientation makes this easier. One advantage reusable services have over previous approaches is their focus on context-free APIs and interfaces implemented using open standards like SOAP and WSDL.

Reusable services can be implemented from scratch or can wrap existing functionality. When creating a brand new component, it can be made more reusable by making it a service—giving it a context-free API and an interface based on open standards, and deploying it such that multiple applications can link to it at deployment-time or runtime. A service may simply wrap functionality that already exists, yet the wrapping still provides value by making the functionality far easier to reuse by a variety of applications, even if they're written in different languages and run on different platforms. A legacy application written in COBOL running on MVS with a copybook interface may be difficult to reuse; but create an adapter for it with a WSDL interface and XSD data structures, and then any Web services client can use it.

The value of reuse-based services has several aspects: Reusable functionality shortens development time by reducing redundant design and development effort and leveraging assets that have already been tested and debugged. By deploying the functionality as a service, it is instantly available to any application that can connect to it. Because it is not embedded in all of those applications, bug fixes and feature enhancements are easier and less disruptive to deploy. Systems encapsulated behind a service interface are easier to later replace or outsource; they're also easier to make available to business partners.

Reusable services fit well into SOA because one of the main goals of SOA is reuse. When two business processes can use the same activity, that's reuse. When two applications need access to the same data, that's reuse. Even when the business people have difficulty identifying reusable business tasks, IT people can usually identify reusable components. Making the reusable components into reusable services makes them part of an SOA.

To start developing a reusable service, look for opportunities for reuse. When multiple applications need the same functionality, make that into a component; and rather than deploying that component embedded in the applications, consider deploying it standalone as a service that the applications link to. When accessing a legacy system, strive to wrap the access code in a service interface that's deployed with the legacy system; then it can be reused by other applications that need to access the legacy system, without each of them having to implement their own access.

Connectivity

The connectivity entry point focuses on providing access to services—regardless of the location of the consumer or provider—via open standards and, when needed, proprietary interfaces. Even when a service is available for reuse, finding it and a way to connect to it can be half the battle. Even if the interfaces match, remote access across networks can be notoriously unreliable. Even with matching interfaces over reliable networks, a service consumer actually needs access to multiple providers of a service, making the service itself reliable and scalable. Even when a consumer knows how to find a provider, the provider may move, in which case the consumer has to be able to find it again.

Service connectivity unites application integration and SOA. Remote process invocation and queued messaging have long been used to enable independent applications to communicate. That integration has now evolved to include service orientation, whereby applications invoke services in each other. The remote process is now a service; the request message is now a command to invoke the service, and its reply message is the result returned by the service. The integration is no longer simply via data exchange, but via service invocation.

Service connectivity is best implemented by an enterprise service bus (ESB) and service registry. An ESB acts like a provider to service consumers and a consumer to service providers. It acts as a single connection point to a consumer, but can connect to multiple providers and route different invocations to different providers. When the consumers and providers don't match, the ESB can perform mediations to bridge the differences. The difference might be in data format bridged by a transformation, transport bridged by a conversion, or purpose bridged by a routing. In the process, the ESB can provide and enforce security and act as a point for management and monitoring—not just of the services or even their individual providers, but at an even more fine-grained level, the individual invocations of the services. Meanwhile, the registry keeps track of the available providers of each service, metadata about the providers, and their current status. The ESB can use the registry to find providers when it needs them.

The value of service connectivity is that a service that cannot be accessed cannot be used. The more complex service access becomes, the more difficult an SOA is to develop and make operate correctly. Service connectivity encapsulates the access, making the means of access reusable, as well as simplifying both the consumers and the providers. It creates a place to implement mediations so that consumers and providers that don't match can still work together. By necessity, service consumers and providers will tend to evolve somewhat independently; as they do, mediations will help bridge the differences.

Service connectivity fits well into SOA because developing service consumers and providers is only half the battle; they need to be connected as well. If every consumer matched its provider and they evolved in lockstep, each consumer had only one provider, the providers' locations and status never changed, and the consumer and provider ran in the same process or at least on the same machine, then service connectivity would be much simpler. But the promise of SOA is that it will work even when interfaces don't match, will enable each consumer to transparently access multiple providers that are not always available, to access them remotely across networks that aren't always reliable, and will enable providers to change their address, old providers to go offline, and new ones to come online. Service connectivity makes this possible; it decouples the consumer from the provider.

To start developing service connectivity, look for services (that is, service providers) that could be reused more if only they were more accessible. Perhaps multiple Java applications running on UNIX servers are having trouble accessing a service hosted on a mainframe, especially because it can become overloaded or sometimes get taken offline. Perhaps a business partner needs controlled, secure access to a service. Maybe a composite application has consumers running in one data center and providers running in a different data center. Perhaps the binding for accessing a needed service changes from time to time. Service connectivity makes services easier to reuse in general, but especially in these more extreme circumstances.

3

Capabilities of an SOA Application Infrastructure

We've looked at why SOA is important and how to get started discovering the services for an SOA application. Now let's look at the capabilities that need to be provided by the infrastructure on which an SOA application runs. Before we discuss the infrastructure, however, we need to review some terminology.

Terminology

SOA builds on component-based architecture, which is a good practice for organizing an application that helps to make it more modular. Services take modularity one step further, not only dividing an application into components, but enabling multiple applications to link to each component at deployment or runtime.

Whereas a component is a unit of code that can be executed to provide functionality, a service is a component that is actually running, often in its own process hosted independently from the applications that are invoking it. Indeed, the applications themselves can be broken into parts that each run in their own process and invoke each other through services.

An application broken into parts like this, where some of them can be shared between applications, is a composite application—"a set of related and integrated services that supports a business process built on an SOA" (IBM's SOA Foundation white paper). A composite application contains two main layers:

1. *Service coordinator*—In a composite application, this is the part that users think of as the application. Although it offers functionality to the user, it implements little functionality itself; rather, it mostly implements service consumers that delegate to service providers. The service coordinator determines which services to invoke when, can use multiple services to implement a unit of user functionality, and stores state between service invocations.

2. *Service providers*—These are implementations of services (discussed below).

A concept related to SOA is the enterprise service bus (ESB), which enables software applications running on different platforms—written in different programming languages and using different programming models—to communicate with each other without requiring expensive, time-consuming reengineering. An ESB enables mediation—routing, transformation, and conversion—to be applied to messages during transmission. It is standards-based, which helps facilitate integrating products from different vendors and avoid an SOA that requires vendor lock-in.

One of the main jobs an ESB performs is connecting together service consumers—also referred to as service requestors, which invoke services—with service providers, which implement services. A service consumer and corresponding service provider share a common service interface, which defines the service's API as a set of related operations, each service operation being a function or method that can execute individually. The ESB implements each service interface (or at least acts like it does) and enables a consumer to invoke the service. The consumer invokes the service as if the architecture has only one provider of that service and the consumer is connected directly to it. The ESB selects among multiple providers of the service and routes the invocation to the selected provider. In this way, the consumers and providers do not need to know about each other; they just need to all connect to the ESB. This is called service virtualization, where a consumer can be served by multiple providers, yet the consumer is not aware of them or which one performs a particular invocation.

A service provider can be implemented as a composite business service, one that implements a service by invoking other services. A composite service can be a long-running service that performs business service choreography (also called service orchestration), which enables the development and execution of business process flow logic, which is centrally controlled and is outside application logic. Service choreography enables multiple services to be run in a specified order and in a coordinated fashion that implements a business process. The business process is itself a service, one that combines simpler services into a long-running flow of services.

SOA Reference Architecture

Now let's look at the infrastructure needed to run an SOA application.

IBM's SOA reference architecture shows the key capabilities that are required for comprehensive, enterprise-wide SOA solutions. It is a vendor-neutral way of looking at and planning the set of services that goes into building an SOA. A runtime environment needs these service capabilities to be able to support SOA applications, as well as to develop, manage, and monitor SOA applications. An organization does not necessarily need all of these capabilities for its first SOA project. The environment is extensible, so that a project can start with just the parts it needs and then expand the environment as its needs increase. The reference architecture is a great tool for laying out roadmaps for pursuing SOA.

The reference architecture defines capabilities, not products. It is vendor-neutral so it does not include or exclude any specific products. However, a vendor with a comprehensive suite of SOA products should have products to address all of these capabilities. The reference architecture also supports an integrated environment of products from different vendors, each product providing some of the architecture's capabilities.

The SOA reference architecture is most easily understood as a picture. Figure 3.1 shows the SOA reference architecture, a conceptual view of the capabilities

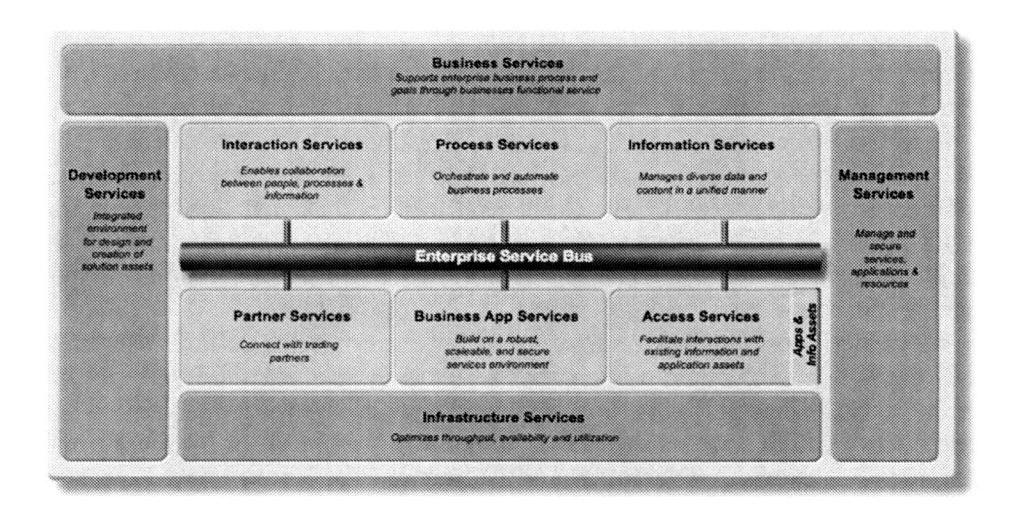

Figure 3.1. SOA reference architecture.

needed to support the development and execution of an SOA application. In the center are six kinds of service providers—interaction, process, information, partner, business application, and access. They all connect via an ESB (described earlier). The service providers are surrounded by capabilities that offer service support. The providers run in an infrastructure that supplies a runtime environment for execution. There are tools for developing the applications and services, tools for managing and monitoring application events, and tools modeling and monitoring business milestones.

Let's look at each of these capabilities in greater detail.

Service Providers

The first set of capabilities includes those for six different kinds of service providers. They are the types of services an enterprise needs for performing business functions. They represent business functionality that has been wrapped into services.

The first three kinds of service providers focus on the integration of people, processes, and information. These services control the flow of interactions and data among people and automated application services in ways appropriate to the realization of a business process. These service types are:

- *Interaction services*—These services enable people to participate in an SOA by using interfaces composed of reusable components, interfaces based on services. They support the integration of users and their devices, as well as ad hoc process composition—such as delegating and forwarding tasks to other users. Products for this capability support creating user interfaces that let people participate in the SOA as consumers that invoke services or by performing tasks in business processes. These services can be discovered using the people entry point, discussed earlier.

- *Process services*—These services automate business processes for common multi-step tasks like creating an account, fulfilling an order, or processing an insurance claim. The automation makes the process less manual and more consistently applied to all customers, and adds traceability and real-time monitoring. People can participate in otherwise automated processes via interaction services. The process can match work to a user profile, making work available to any user fitting the profile and showing a user all work available for his profile. These services also include capabilities for business rules and for state machines. These services can be discovered using the process entry point, discussed earlier.

Business process is implemented through business service choreography and orchestration, also commonly called workflow. It implements long-running services as processes containing activities that are finer-grained services, where the work can proceed in parallel branches, can be transactional and persistent, and can roll back, optionally via compensating transactions. This means that if the system crashes while the business process is running, the process can restart where it was and finish successfully.

- *Information services*—These services offer a single, consistent point of access to timely, accurate, and integrated data—including master data. Any necessary conversions to the data—integration, cleansing, enrichment, etc.—occur transparently behind the service interface, decoupling the consumers from the databases' schemas and locations. Various database and data types—relational, hierarchical, and object, as well as unstructured data—get consistent interfaces for access. Monitoring adds traceability of what data is being used and by whom. These services can be discovered using the information entry point, discussed earlier.

The remaining three kinds of service providers focus on connecting to existing functionality, be it hosted by external partners, newly implemented components, or existing applications. These services encapsulate and automate business logic to make it reusable and consistently applied. They can be discovered using the reuse entry point, discussed earlier. These service types are:

- *Partner services*—These services enable business partners to participate in your enterprise's SOA by providing functionality that your business processes consume. Integrating the systems of the partners and suppliers with those of the enterprise improves efficiency of the overall value chain. These services provide the document, protocol, and partner management capabilities required for efficient implementation of business-to-business processes that involve interactions with outside partners and suppliers.

- *Business application services*—These services enable new application components to be included as part of the SOA environment. These components implement traditional application functionality for new and changing business logic and functionality, which needs to be updated as the business environment evolves. Developing these components into services makes them more reusable, especially by new and updated business processes.

- *Access services*—These services enable access to existing enterprise applications, so-called enterprise information systems like legacy systems, packaged applications, and applications embedded in custom hardware like assembly lines and cash registers. The services also can detect and respond to events from these applications. Developing services for accessing this functionality enables it to be reused by business processes, and to trigger services and processes. These services are often implemented as reusable adapters that simply need to be configured.

Service Connectivity

The second set of capabilities includes those to easily access and invoke the service providers. Connectivity consists of two parts: buses that connect consumers to providers, and registries that keep track of the providers available. They can be discovered using the connectivity entry point, discussed earlier. Here are more details about these two capabilities:

- *Service Bus*—This is the ESB, the backbone of the reference architecture that facilitates communication between services. It connects service consumers to service providers, thereby simplifying access to the services. It acts as a provider to a consumer, as a consumer to a provider, and can connect consumers of a service to multiple providers of that service.

This ESB capability encompasses several finer-grained capabilities:

- *Integration*—This is the ESB's capability to facilitate integrating components and applications, making ones that were not designed to be interoperable nevertheless appear to be so. The ESB does so by implementing the interface each component or application requires so they can connect to the ESB very easily. When the interfaces don't match each other, the ESB can still connect them together using mediations.

- *Mediation*—This is the ESB's capability to intervene between a service consumer and service provider, to change the service invocation as it travels through the bus, thereby connecting incompatible interfaces. An ESB can provide three kinds of mediation: routing, transforming, and converting.

Any service provided by an ESB can use any combination of mediations, including none at all.

Mediation can be a single atomic task applied to a message, such as transforming its format. But it's often a series of tasks, such as: convert a message's transport, validate its format, transform its format, enhance its content with additional data, and finally route it to a more specific kind of receiver. Thus an ESB should provide the capability for mediation flows, a mediation implemented as a series of one or more mediation primitives. An ESB should also include a set of basic mediation primitives, pre-built components for creating custom mediation flows. Since no set of pre-built mediation primitives is ever complete, an ESB should also include a capability for developers to create their own custom mediation primitives.

- *Distribution*—The ESB can facilitate event notification by transmitting events and notifying handlers. The ESB ensures that handlers interested in a category of events will be notified of each event. It can also apply mediations to the event.

- *Service registry*—A registry is a directory of services that keeps track of the service providers, including what service each provider implements, the address and protocol for invoking it, and its current availability. The registry lists the services that are available and the individual providers of the services, and perhaps metadata about the providers. Providers can easily be considered or ignored for receiving service invocations simply by adding them to or removing them from the registry.

Service Support

The third set of capabilities includes those needed to develop, run, manage, and monitor the services:

- *Infrastructure services*—These capabilities form the foundation for executing SOA applications, making services easier to implement and more ro-

More on the Web

ESB Without Limits:
SOA Within Your Grasp

Webcast
Duration 60 minutes
Registration required

(soa.maxpress.com)

bust. They provide a high performance, high throughput, and flexible environment with quality-of-service capabilities like:

- *Virtualization*—Including heterogeneous platforms and clustering

- *Workload management*—Including load balancing

- *High availability*—Including transactions and failover.

These services also provide basic capabilities like data persistence and messaging, often by connecting to external database and messaging systems.

- *Development services*—Being able to run and manage composite applications in production is not enough; it's also necessary to develop and test them first. Tools are an essential component of any comprehensive integration architecture. These services are used to implement custom artifacts that leverage the infrastructure capabilities and assemble them into applications. Tools differ based on the kinds of assets they help develop and the role and skills required of the user, but all must help people from different roles collaborate. Developers need an integrated development environment (IDE) that facilitates:

  - *Modeling*—Design of business processes, business rules, and state machines

  - *Implementation*—Design of service interfaces and implementation of components for service providers and service consumers

  - *Integration*—Wiring together of service consumers to service providers and of business process activities to service providers, configuration of adapters, and development of mediations

  - *Testing*—Execution and testing of components and integrations using integrated test environments that emulate production environments

  - *Asset management*—Configuration management and safekeeping of development artifacts, as well as problem tracking and the resulting artifact changes.

- *Management services*—These services provide for management, monitoring, and security of IT resources, services, and composite applications.

Resources to be managed include application servers, database servers, Web servers, server computers, and networks. This includes:

- *Security*—Including basic authentication, access control, and encryption

- *IT monitoring*—Capabilities to observe the resources to ensure they're running properly

- *Service management*—Capabilities to adjust the application parts while they're running, including automated capabilities to take corrective action when problems occur, applied at the level not just of composite applications as a whole but also of individual services

- *Policy*—Rules and parameters to determine proper functioning and to specify corrective action, including when and how to notify IT administrators of failures

• *Business services*—These services provide for modeling, monitoring, and improvement not at the level of the IT components the applications run in but at the level of the business functions the system performs. Together, they form a business-focused approach that helps to develop innovative, optimized, flexible business process models that can be deployed quickly and whose performance can be measured to drive improvement. This includes:

- *Business modeling*—An analyst designs business processes describing key functions that the enterprise performs. These processes can be run as simulations including delays which show visually and statistically how long tasks take and where the bottlenecks occur. The analyst can use these simulations to improve the process and test those improvements. The refined models can then be used by developers as the basis of the business processes for process services.

- *Business monitoring*—Simulations are nice, but they don't necessarily model reality; models running in production can't avoid reflecting reality. Monitoring of production systems keeps statistics on how long activities take to run and which end up blocked waiting on others. Those statistics show inaccuracies in the model; the analyst can feed those statistics back into the model to improve the accuracy of the simulation. The analyst, discovering where the bottlenecks really are, may ask development what they can do to improve the efficiency of a key service's implementation.

- *Business dashboards*—Executives need statistics on how their business is running—metrics like accounts opened, products built, orders shipped, support cases handled, returns received—to adjust the business and make it run more effectively, especially under changing conditions. Too often, executives are making decisions based on information that is incomplete, stale, and conflicting. A business dashboard is designed to specifically gather, correlate, and display business event metrics that show executives how their business is running in real time. The dashboards gather their metrics from the business processes using the monitoring of the business models as they are running in production.

One key feature of the SOA reference architecture is the linkage between the development services and the business services. Runtime data and statistics fed into the modeling environment enable analysis, which drives iterative process reengineering, which then feeds into development and deployment of improved business processes, which then generates new runtime data and statistics.

Standards Driven

In addition to its component model, another focus of the SOA reference architecture is its basis on open standards like XML, SOAP, WSDL, and JMS. An open standard is developed cooperatively by a range of vendors and is ratified by a neutral body. A standard specifies what a technology must do but not how it must do it. This enables users to rely on the what while vendors compete on the how.

One of the main goals of SOA is to be able to integrate together services implemented in different technologies such as language and platform. For this to be possible, the parts have to agree on how they will connect and talk to each other; their implementation can differ but their interfaces must be compatible. In SOA, this is the question of how the service interfaces are expressed and of how the consumers invoke the providers through these interfaces. These interfaces and the invocation mechanisms must match in order for a consumer to invoke a provider. When these interfaces and mechanisms are designed following the same standard, they become more interoperable and can much more easily work together, which speeds development and lowers risk.

4

Products for an SOA Application Infrastructure

So far, we've looked at how to get started with SOA and the execution environment needed to run SOA applications. Now let's look at the products IBM offers to build that SOA runtime environment. We'll also look in detail at the capabilities of IBM's main SOA application server product, WebSphere Process Server. And we'll quickly review the professional consulting services available from IBM to help organizations adopt SOA.

Products for the SOA Reference Architecture

The SOA reference architecture, illustrated earlier in Figure 3.1, shows the capabilities required for comprehensive, enterprise-wide SOA solutions. It is vendor-neutral, showing the capabilities an SOA environment needs without specifying what products to use to implement it. But the architecture is just that—a plan; it cannot be installed or used in production. A production environment requires products that implement the capabilities specified by the architecture.

This section reviews products IBM offers to realize the SOA reference architecture. Figure 4.1 shows the SOA reference architecture again, this time labeled with the names of IBM products. This provides an overview of the IBM products an enterprise can use to create its own installation of the reference architecture environment.

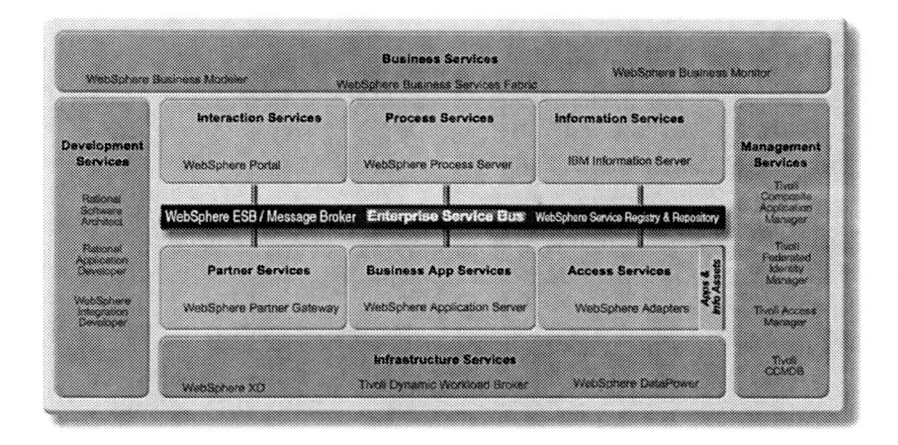

Figure 4.1. Products for the SOA reference architecture.

The diagram illustrates IBM's comprehensive suite of products for providing all capabilities needed in a complete SOA architecture. Different capabilities are provided by separate products, so an enterprise's first SOA projects require only the products for the capabilities needed. Sometimes an enterprise may choose to use a non-IBM product to achieve a capability; as long as the product follows open standards, it should still fit into the reference architecture and work compatibly with the IBM products.

Let's look at the products for each of these capabilities in greater detail.

Products for SOA Infrastructure

Infrastructure services provide the foundation for executing SOA applications, providing a high-performance, high-throughput, and flexible environment with quality-of-service capabilities. These are the main products IBM offers that form this foundation:

- *WebSphere Extended Deployment*—Provides a dynamic, goals-directed, high-performance environment for running mixed-application types and workload patterns in WebSphere. It optimizes hardware utilization by dynamically adjusting capacity where it is needed most based on user demand and administrator-configured policies and service level agreements (SLAs). Based on application load measurements, it increases capacity for applications

> **More on the Web**
>
> - WebSphere Extended Deployment
> - Enhanced Infrastructure Capabilities for SOA Environments
> - Tivoli Dynamic Workload Broker
> - Configuring Tivoli Dynamic Workload Broker and EWLW for Efficient Job Dispatching and Scheduling
> - WebSphere Datapower SOA Appliances
> - Making SOA Real with WebSphere
>
> *(soa.maxpress.com)*

currently experiencing high demand or exceeding acceptable response times by lowering capacity for lower-demand or lower-priority applications. It includes these capabilities: dynamic operations, ObjectGrid, on demand router (ODR), partitioning facility, visualization, geographic workload management, business grid, and application edition manager.

- *Tivoli Dynamic Workload Broker*—Creates a virtualized environment on an existing infrastructure, which enables it to automatically adapt job execution to environmental changes, distributing workloads to the best available resources within a changing infrastructure.

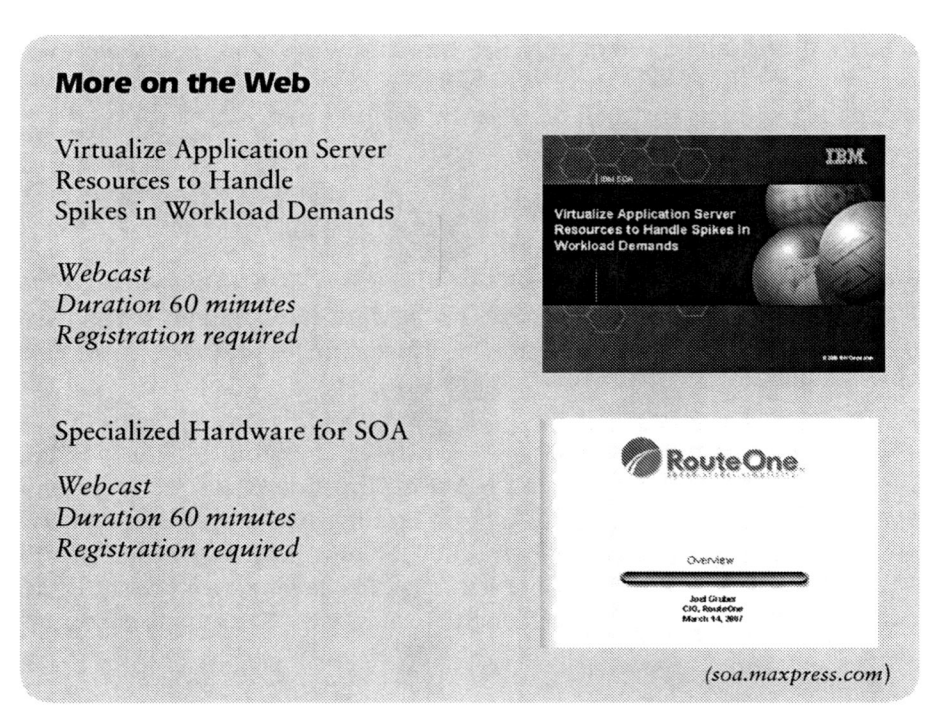

> **More on the Web**
>
> Virtualize Application Server Resources to Handle Spikes in Workload Demands
>
> *Webcast*
> *Duration 60 minutes*
> *Registration required*
>
> Specialized Hardware for SOA
>
> *Webcast*
> *Duration 60 minutes*
> *Registration required*
>
> *(soa.maxpress.com)*

- *WebSphere Datapower SOA Appliances*—Specialized network devices optimized to accelerate processing of XML and Web services messages, enforce security, and integrate with other data formats. These serve as gateways to an ESB, forming an outer layer of integration logic around the ESB that performs authorization, one-to-one transformations, and basic routing. This device integrates with WebSphere Service Registry and Repository and with WebSphere Transformation Extender. There are three models: the XA35 XML Accelerator, the XS40 XML Security Gateway, and the XI50 Integration Appliance.

Products for Human Interaction with SOA

Interaction services enable people to participate in an SOA, supporting the integration of users and their devices, as well as ad hoc process composition. The main IBM product that supports interaction services is:

- *WebSphere Portal*—Web portals provide users with a single, personalized access point to Web content and applications. IBM WebSphere Portal includes support for workflows, content management, simplified usability and administration, open standards, security, and scalability. A portal is composed of portlets, pluggable user interface components that make a reusable service available to a user.

> **More on the Web**
>
> - WebSphere Portal from WebSphere
> - New to WebSphere Portal
>
> *(soa.maxpress.com)*

Products for SOA Business Process Management

Process services enable automation of business processes, decomposing long-running tasks into finer-grained, reusable activities that are also services. Activities that cannot be automated can be performed as interaction services and still be managed by the business process. The main IBM product that supports process services is:

- *WebSphere Process Server*—The WebSphere SOA application server

> **More on the Web**
>
> - WebSphere Process Server
> - New to WebSphere Business Integration
> - WebSphere Process Server: IBM's New Foundation for SOA
>
> *(soa.maxpress.com)*

is a comprehensive integration platform built on top of WebSphere Application Server. Its capabilities support the development and execution of SOA applications with business integration components based on open standards. *Process Server* is covered in depth later.

Products for Information as a Service

Information services offer a single point of access for common data functions. Data integration, cleansing, and transformation occur transparently behind the service interface, decoupling the consumers from the databases' locations and schemas. The main IBM product that supports information services is:

- *IBM Information Server*—Creates consistent, reusable SOA information services that present a business view spanning across diverse sources. This is a platform for information integration with several different optional modules, including WebSphere Federation Server, WebSphere Information Services Director, WebSphere DataStage, WebSphere QualityStage, WebSphere Business Glossary, and WebSphere Information Analyzer.

> **More on the Web**
>
> - IBM Information Server
> - IBM DeveloperWorks Information Integration Zone
> - Bob Zurek on IBM Information Server
>
> *(soa.maxpress.com)*

Products for Partner Services

Partner services enable an enterprise's business processes to reuse functionality running in business partners' systems. These services provide the document, protocol, and partner management capabilities required for efficient implementation of business-to-business processes that involve interactions with outside partners and suppliers. The main IBM product that supports partner services is:

- *WebSphere Partner Gateway*—Provides a consolidated access point for B2B integration with business partners. It provides centralized management of all external interactions, including partner management, security, and service-level agreements. It supports communication with non-repudiation via

> **More on the Web**
>
> - WebSphere Partner Gateway
> - WebSphere Partner Gateway, Version 6.0
>
> *(soa.maxpress.com)*

multiple B2B protocols and standards, including traditional EDI and FTP scripting for VAN connectivity, as well as XML-based data formats and Internet standard transports.

Products for Business Application Services

Business application services enable new application components to be included as part of the SOA environment. Developing these components into services makes them more reusable, especially by new and updated business processes. The main IBM product that supports business application services is:

- *WebSphere Application Server*—The application server for the WebSphere brand delivers the secure, scalable, resilient application infrastructure that is ideal for hosting services that are implemented with the Java 2 Enterprise Edition (J2EE) programming model. For example, a service can be implemented as a stateless session bean, a type of Enterprise JavaBean (EJB).

> **More on the Web**
>
> - WebSphere Application Server
> - New to WebSphere Application Server
>
> (soa.maxpress.com)

Products for SOA Access to Existing Applications

Access services enable access to existing enterprise applications as well as detecting events from these applications. The main IBM products that support access services are:

- *WebSphere Adapters*—These make legacy applications act like service providers without needing to change the application. They access functionality in an existing application so that it can be invoked as a service and detect events in the applications that can trigger the invocation of other services. In this way, applications that were never designed to be part of an SOA can nevertheless participate in one without costly redevelopment. Many of the adapters are J2EE Connector Architecture compatible.

> **More on the Web**
>
> - WebSphere Adapters
> - Connect Data and Applications Across Your Enterprise
>
> (soa.maxpress.com)

Products for Service Connectivity

Service connectivity consists of the enterprise service bus and the service registry. The enterprise service bus is the backbone of the reference architecture, which facilitates communication between services, connecting service consumers to service providers and optionally applying mediations during a service invocation. The service registry is a directory of the services available, the providers of those services, and how to invoke them. IBM products that support service connectivity include:

- *WebSphere Enterprise Service Bus*—Provides Web services connectivity, JMS messaging, and service oriented integration for SOA connectivity. A product implementation of the ESB pattern, it provides a mediation framework for performing message routing, format transformation, and transport conversion. Its mediations are implemented as mediation flows using the service component architecture (SCA) framework. WebSphere ESB embeds WebSphere Application Server and is embedded in WebSphere Process Server, as discussed in the later section "WebSphere Process Server Component Model." WebSphere ESB integrates with WebSphere Service Registry and Repository and with WebSphere Transformation Extender.

- *WebSphere Message Broker*—Delivers an ESB that provides connectivity and universal data transformation for both standards- and non-standards-based applications and services for SOA connectivity. A product implementation of the ESB pattern, it provides a mediation framework for performing message routing, format transformation, and transport conversion. Message broker mediations are implemented as mediation flows with nodes implemented using ESQL, Java, and message maps. It includes the Message Broker Toolkit for developing message flows. It integrates

More on the Web

- Enterprise Service Bus
- WebSphere Enterprise Service Bus
- IBM developerWorks WebSphere Enterprise Service Bus Zone
- WebSphere Transformation Extender
- WebSphere Transformation Extender: Solve Complex Data Challanges
- WebSphere Message Broker
- IBM developerWorks WebSphere Message Broker Zone
- WebSphere Service Registry and Repository
- Introducing IBM WebSphere Service Registry and Repository

(soa.maxpress.com)

with WebSphere Service Registry and Repository and with WebSphere Transformation Extender.

- *WebSphere Service Registry and Repository*—This is a repository for service definitions and a registry for providers of those services. It provides a centralized directory for developers to find the services available for reuse, and is used by service consumers and ESBs at runtime to find providers and the addresses for invoking them. Service Registry and Repository is an important tool for management and governance of services, described in detail in the later section "SOA Governance." WebSphere ESB, Message Broker, and Datapower can all use Registry and Repository to discover service providers at runtime.

Products for SOA Development

Development services enable staff to architect, design, implement, and test composite applications to be deployed into the rest of the SOA reference architecture. Various integrated development environments (IDEs) are specialized for various development roles and to produce artifacts to be deployed into different runtime products. IBM products that support development services include:

- *WebSphere Integration Developer*—This is the development IDE for WebSphere Process Server and WebSphere Enterprise Service Bus, built on the Eclipse platform. It is intended for use by integration developers, those who focus on wiring together service consumers and providers. It has tools for developing service component architecture (SCA) modules, including editors for BPEL business processes, business rules, interface maps, and other Process Server features, as well as mediation flows for WebSphere ESB.

More on the Web

- WebSphere Integration Developer
- IBM developerWorks WebSphere Process Server and WebSphere Integration Devloper Zone
- Rational Application Developer for WebSphere Software
- IBM developerWorks Rational Application Developer for WebSphere Software Zone
- Rational Software Architect
- IBM developerWorks Rational Sotware Architect Zone

(soa.maxpress.com)

- *Rational Application Developer for WebSphere Software*—This is the development IDE for WebSphere Application Server, built on the Eclipse platform. It is intended for use by programmers whose focus is on writing Java Enterprise Edition components using Java code. It helps them rapidly design, develop, assemble, test, profile, and deploy high-quality Java, Portal, Web, Web services, and SOA applications.

- *Rational Software Architect*—This development IDE does what Application Developer does, plus adds tools for model-driven development (MDD). It is intended for use by architects to create the high-level design of the major components in an application. It has tools for developing UML models, including tools to generate Java code from the models through model-to-model and model-to-code transformations.

Products for SOA Management

Management services provide for management, monitoring, and security of IT resources, services, and composite applications. They help ensure that the systems are running properly, log status, take corrective action when a problem is detected, and alert administrators when corrective actions fail. IBM products that support management services fit into three categories: service management, service security, and configuration management.

Service Management

These are the services that manage and monitor the IT systems. The main IBM product that supports service management is:

- *Tivoli Composite Application Manager for SOA*—ITCAM for SOA will monitor, manage, and control SOAs deployed using a wide range of systems from IBM and other vendors. It can help with service availability, service performance, service load management, service level reporting, and service visualization.

More on the Web

- Tivoli Composite Application Management
- IBM Tivoli Composite Application Manager for SOA
- IBM develperWorks Composite Application Management zone
- SOA Foundation, Part 3: Managing and monitoring your SOA

(soa.maxpress.com)

Service Security

These are the services that manage the security of the IT systems. IBM products that support service security include:

- *Tivoli Federated Identity Manager*—FIM enables organizations to share identity and policy data about users and services, including policy-based integrated security management for federated Web services. It enables loose coupling of disparate identity management systems and avoids replication of identity and security administration at multiple enterprises.

- *Tivoli Access Manager for e-business*—One of several Tivoli Access Manager products, this one provides authentication and authorization for Web applications, including single sign-on (SSO). It provides a centralized point to define and manage authentication, access, and audit policies, enabling and controlling user access between applications.

Configuration Management

These are the services that manage the code and other assets for implementing the services. The main IBM product for this purpose is:

- *Tivoli Change and Configuration Management Database*—CCMDB provides an enterprise-ready platform for storing deep, standardized data on configurations and change histories to help integrate people, processes, information, and technology. It helps with SOA governance by enabling better anticipation of the impact of changes, lowering the business risks of service failures and inconsistencies. (See the later section, "SOA Governance.")

> **More on the Web**
>
> - Tivoli Federated Identity Manager
> - Tivoli Federated Identity Manager Business Gateway
> - Tivoli Access Manager for e-business
> - Tivoli Change and Configuration Management Database
>
> *(soa.maxpress.com)*

Products for Business Services

Business services enable staff to model, monitor, and improve business processes at the level of business functionality and business metrics (and not get lost in the details of the IT infrastructure the system runs on). Products in this category go together to model reality and then measure the model's accuracy in order to improve the model. IBM products that support business innovation and optimization services include:

> **More on the Web**
>
> - WebSphere Business Modeler
> - IBM developerWorks WebSphere Business Integration Zone
> - WebSphere Business Monitor
> - An End-to-end Solution Using WebSphere Buiness Integration v6.0
> - WebSphere Business Services Fabric
> - Business Services Fabric: An Industry View of SOA
>
> *(soa.maxpress.com)*

- *WebSphere Business Modeler*—Makes business analysis more productive by providing a modeling and test environment for business processes. Analysts can model and visualize key business processes without getting lost in the details of how they will be implemented, and they can add milestones for monitoring. Business Modeler enables simulation of the model to discover bottlenecks and test candidate optimizations, and to try "What if?" scenarios to learn how the business might operate better. It interoperates with WebSphere Business Monitor.

- *WebSphere Business Monitor*—Enables measurement of the business while it's operating by capturing and evaluating key business activity events. Business Monitor takes the guesswork out of wondering how business processes run, how long activities take, and where bottlenecks exist—by showing real metrics of actual running business processes. It interoperates with WebSphere Business Modeler to define milestones to measure and to feed measurements back into the model.

- *WebSphere Business Services Fabric*—An end-to-end platform for the modeling, assembly, deployment, management, and governance of composite business services in an SOA. Business-level services can be assembled into extended, cross-enterprise business processes and solutions that are dynamically personalized and delivered based on the business context of the service request.

WebSphere Process Server Component Model

Having explored the products for each capability in the SOA reference architecture, let's now focus on WebSphere Process Server, which embodies a core set of SOA capabilities.

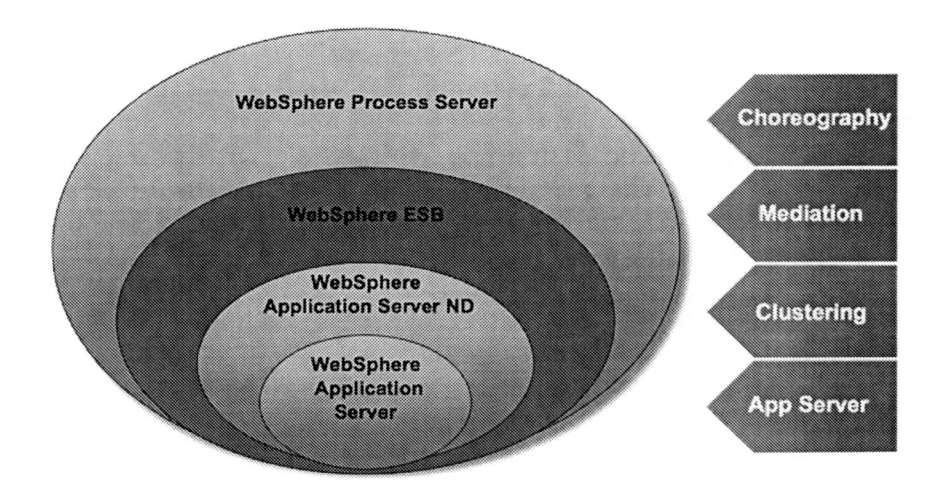

Figure 4.2. Products embedded in WebSphere Process Server.

Process Server Embedded Products

WebSphere Process Server contains several other WebSphere products within it. It is also closely related to the development product used to create its applications.

We'll start by exploring how WebSphere Process Server contains a couple of other runtime server products from IBM. Figure 4.2 shows the products that are embedded inside of WebSphere Process Server and the features that they add.

There are four products which work together to create the four layers of functionality. We have already discussed WebSphere Application Server, WebSphere Enterprise Service Bus, and WebSphere Process Server individually. Now let's see how these products together create the functionality contained in WebSphere Process Server.

- *WebSphere Application Server*—This is a single application server. It implements the runtime portion of the Java 2 Enterprise Edition (J2EE) specification and can run any application that complies with the J2EE programming model. It includes the service integration bus, a built-in Java Message Service (JMS) provider.

- *WebSphere Application Server Network Deployment*—This adds clustering to WebSphere Application Server (base). Whereas the base product runs a single application server on a single host machine, Network Deployment can run multiple application servers on one or more host machines, and can cluster them to make them act like one huge application server with much greater scalability and reliability. One way for applications to communicate between application servers is using the service integration bus.

- *WebSphere Enterprise Service Bus*—This adds ESB functionality—integration, mediation, and distribution—to Network Deployment. Its buses run on top of the service integration bus. It includes pre-built mediation primitives and the ability to implement custom primitives. Mediation flows are implemented using the service component architecture (SCA).

- *WebSphere Process Server*—This adds service choreography to WebSphere ESB. Choreography provides the ability to run multiple services in a coordinated, orchestrated fashion. This is implemented in Process Server by its Business Process Choreographer (BPC) feature, which is a BPEL (business process) engine. SOA components in Process Server, including BPEL processes, are implemented using the service component architecture (SCA).

This means that Process Server is an SOA platform with a built-in ESB. Process Server has WebSphere ESB built in, and WebSphere ESB has Application Server built in. One can deploy J2EE applications to Process Server or WebSphere ESB and they'll run just fine, although Application Server is the more cost-effective alternative. More importantly, an SOA application deployed to Process Server doesn't require a separate ESB; it can use the ESB that's already built into Process Server, which is the full WebSphere ESB product.

Process Server is also closely related with the development product used to create its applications. Not only are Process Server and WebSphere ESB closely related, but they're both closely related with WebSphere Integration Developer (discussed in the earlier section). Integration Developer is the integrated development environment (IDE) specifically designed for Process Server and WebSphere ESB. Just as those runtime platforms execute service component architecture (SCA) components, Integration Developer is specifically designed for implementing SCA components. Integration Developer contains test servers for both Process Server and WebSphere ESB so developers can test and debug their components from within their development environment.

Process Server Component Model

Now that we've reviewed the products embedded into and associated with WebSphere Process Server, let's look at the parts of Process Server, because these parts define the capabilities it can bring to an SOA application. Figure 4.3 shows the component model in Process Server, which shows the main features it makes available for SOA.

Products for an SOA Application Infrastructure

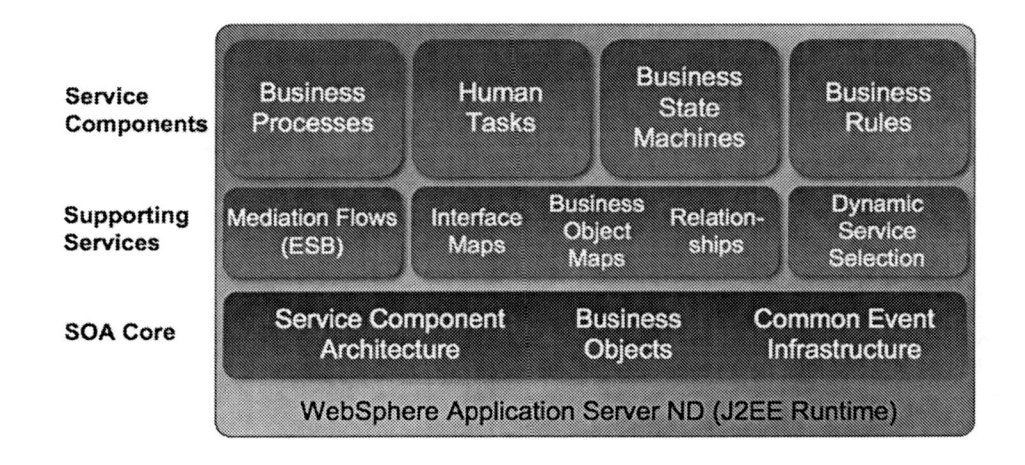

Figure 4.3. WebSphere Process Server component model.

These components form three layers of functionality:

- *SOA core*—This is the foundation for SOA functionality, a simplified programming model for SOA.

- *Supporting services*—These are technical services used to glue business services together. Ideally, business services should be designed to work together—the consumers should match the providers—but often they do not, and so these supporting services are needed as adapters to make the business services fit together.

- *Service components*—These are technical capabilities to implement business services using higher programming models that don't require writing code in a traditional programming language like Java. Integration developers should be able to "program" at this level.

Let's explore these features in detail.

SOA Core

First, let's look at the components that are common to both Process Server and WebSphere ESB. Since Process Server is built on top of WebSphere ESB, this first set of components includes the capabilities in WebSphere ESB.

> **More on the Web**
>
> - Common Event Infrastructure
> - Common Base Event Specification
> - IBM and Cisco Collaborate on Automatic Computing Solutions
> - Standardize Messages with the Common Base Event Model
> - Service Component Architecture
> - Open Service Oriented Architecture Collaboration
> - SCA at OASIS
> - Apache Tuscany
>
> *(soa.maxpress.com)*

- *WebSphere Application Server Network Deployment*—As already discussed, WebSphere ESB is built on top of Network Deployment. This provides a standards-based, high-performance environment for the ESB and the applications that use it.

- *Service Component Architecture*—SCA is a service invocation, componentization, and programming model specifically for SOA.

- *Business Objects*—This is a format for data exchange between service components, based on Service Data Objects (SDO).

- *Common Event Infrastructure*—CEI is a foundation for business observation, which is monitoring of SOA applications and using those insights to understand what is happening in the business. It produces events that conform to the Common Base Event specification.

Service Component Architecture (SCA) and Service Data Objects (SDO) are proprietary specifications that are being developed into standards; the SDO standard should include the functionality in business objects. IBM created SCA, its specification, and its implementation in WebSphere Process Server. The specifications for SCA and SDO are now owned by the Open Service Oriented Architecture (OSOA) collaboration, of which IBM is a member, which has further developed these specifications and submitted them to OASIS for standardization. Meanwhile, the Apache Tuscany project, to which IBM is a contributor, is developing open-source implementations of the OSOA specifications in several languages, including Java and C++. The Eclipse SOA Tools Platform project, to which IBM is a contributor, is developing open-source tooling for implementing SCA components.

Supporting Services

Secondly, now that we've looked at the components that are common to both Process Server and WebSphere ESB, let's look at the components that are only in Process Server, those that Process Server adds to WebSphere ESB.

Supporting service components do not implement services, but rather provide capabilities to integrate existing services—that is, to make them work together—and to select one service provider among many. These components are:

- *Mediation flows*—We've discussed mediations in the earlier section "Service Connectivity"; they perform logic on messages flowing through the ESB, intervening between a service consumer and service provider. In WebSphere ESB, mediation is implemented as a mediation flow, which can be a single task or a series of tasks, where each task is a mediation primitive. WebSphere ESB and Integration Developer come stocked with pre-built mediation primitives for tasks like filtering, logging, endpoint lookup in WebSphere Services Registry and Repository, and XSL transformations. Developers can also implement their own custom mediation primitives.

Like the SOA core capabilities, mediation flows is a capability included in WebSphere ESB. It's grouped as a supporting service component because it is used to integrate existing services.

- *Interface maps*—These maps adapt one service syntax to another. Sometimes services that perform the same function do not call it the same thing; they still can be used together, but a map has to adapt the interface the provider implements to the one the consumer expects. An interface map enables these consumers and providers to work together and doesn't require the developer to write any code.

- *Business object maps*—These maps adapt one service data format to another. Sometimes services that need the same data don't format it the same or encapsulate it as different types; they still can be used together, but a map has to transform the data the consumer passes out into the data the provider accepts. For example, the consumer in one application may define an address record one way, whereas the provider in another application defines address differently. The applications may agree on an "Address::get Address(CustomerID)" operation, but the address record has to be transformed. A business object map enables the consumer and provider to work together and doesn't require the developer to write any code.

> **More on the Web**
>
> - Getting Started with WebSphere Enterprise Service Bus and WebSphere Integration Developer
> - WebSphere Process Server relationship service, Part 1: Static relationships
> - WebSphere Process Server relationship service, Part 2:Dynamic relationships
>
> *(soa.maxpress.com)*

- *Relationships*—These convert one data store's keys to another's. For example, two systems—billing and inventory—should contain the same order records and product records, but they probably will have different unique IDs for the same records. A query between systems may specify just an order ID, or an order record passed between systems may contain product IDs. Because the IDs are different between the systems, they must be mapped. Similarly, one system may represent the name of a state with the full name like "New York," whereas another system uses an abbreviation like "NY." A relationship can be static or dynamic. A relationship enables such a consumer and provider to work together and doesn't require the developer to write any code. Interface maps, business object maps, and relationships all go together; the first construct contains the latter two. Business services communicate through interfaces, so if they need to be glued together, this must be done through their interface. Thus, a provider and its consumer cannot be glued together using a business object map or relationship; the gluing must always be performed by an interface map, even if the consumer's and provider's operation names and parameter orders match. The interface map can, in turn, use business object maps and relationships as needed to convert the parameters. Such a combination of mappings can be modeled in Integration Developer and executed in Process Server.

- *Dynamic service selection*—This chooses which of multiple components with the same interface to invoke. Different implementations of the same service interface can customize functionality for different circumstances, such as gold customers versus not, in-season versus out-of-season, or multiple legal jurisdictions. A selector can be used to choose among these options so that the consumer thinks they're all just one option. Selection decisions can be implemented as another component, such as business rules (discussed below). There are built-in selection criteria for date range, integer range, and string matching (e.g., enumeration); also, developers can implement custom selectors with their own criteria. A selector can be changed at runtime without restarting the server, providing the ability to dynamically adjust the application while it's in use. A selector might even be "hard coded" to always use the same component, but then can be changed to always use a different component, and the change can be made while the system is running.

Service Components

Thirdly, now that we've looked at basic functionality for implementing services and capabilities for integrating them, let's look at capabilities that provide higher-level programming models for implementing services.

- *Business processes*—These execute Business Process Execution Language (BPEL) business processes for service choreography. The BPEL business process engine in Process Server is called the Business Process Choreographer (BPC). Business service choreography enables the automation of business process flow logic, extracting the logic from the underlying applications to make it more easily understood, modified, and monitored. Business process automation is a key part of the SOA value proposition because it enables an enterprise to quickly develop new services using existing services and components.

BPEL standardizes workflow. It expresses a business process in a standardized format supported by multiple vendors, so it avoids vendor lock-in. A process can be modeled in one vendor's editor and exported as BPEL, then imported and executed in a different vendor's engine. One shortcoming of the current BPEL standard is that it supports only processes that are completely automated; it does not support human interaction.

More on the Web

- Business Process Execution Language for Web Services (WS-BPEL)
- Using BPEL and EJBs with WebSphere Process Server and WebSphere Integration Developer
- IBM developerWorks and Business Process Choreographer Zone
- SOA Programming Model for implementing Web services, Part 8: Human-based Web Services
- WS-BPEL Extension for People (WBEL4People)
- WebSphere Process Server Business State Machines Concepts and Capabilities
- Creating and Deploying Business Rules

(soa.maxpress.com)

- *Human tasks*—These enable people to invoke business processes and perform business process activities. Although BPEL does not support human interaction, Process Server has additional functionality beyond BPEL that does. Human tasks are service components just like any other and so can be used to implement any service. Human tasks can be used to model escalations, such as an overdue task or one requiring approval. The human task manager is based on the emerging standard WS-BPEL Extension for People (BPEL4People).

- *Business state machines*—These model a business process as a finite set of states and event transitions. This is an alternative way to model how a process is performed by focusing not on the activities that need to be performed, but on the states that need to be reached and the transitions that can be used to reach them. For example, an insurance claim may have states like submitted, verified, approved, and denied; a transition from submitted to verified may be research. Some processes are more easily modeled as activities, others as state machines; Process Server offers both approaches.

- *Business rules*—These are rule sets and decision tables for simple decision making. Business rules complement business processes and state machines; whereas those first two focus on tasks and status, rules model making decisions for what should be done next. The execution of rules includes the current context; for example, the context includes the current date so that rules can automatically adjust based on time or calendar. Rules can be edited and updated while the application is in use. One rules editor is the template editor, a Web-based management tool business analysts can use to adjust rules in a natural, non-programmatic way.

Professional Services for SOA Adoption

So far, we've discussed the software products IBM offers for building the runtime infrastructure described in the "SOA Reference Architecture." IBM also offers professional services, consultants who can help an organization adopt SOA. Professional services experts act as guides who know how to successfully make the transition to SOA; they can help perform necessary tasks, mentor teams on how to perform the

> **More on the Web**
>
> - SOA Consulting Services
> - SOA Business Services
> - SOA Infrastructure Services
> - SOA Software Services
>
> (soa.maxpress.com)

> **More on the Web**
>
> Prevent IT Paralysis—
> Seek the Flexible IT Cure
>
> *Webcast*
> *Duration 60 minutes*
> *Registration required*
>
> (soa.maxpress.com)

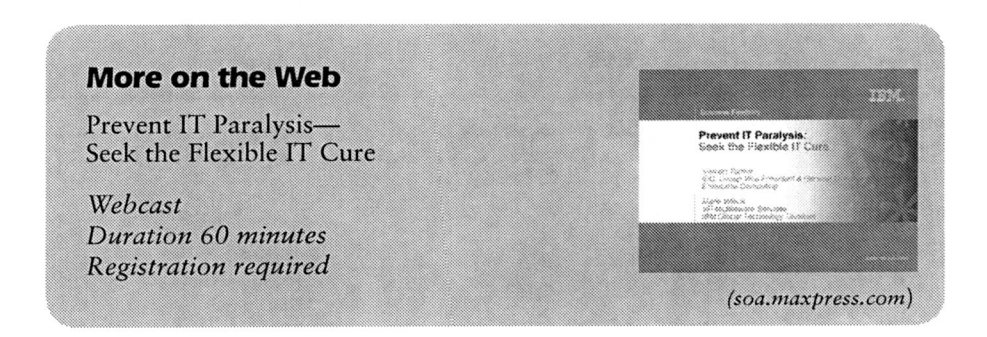

tasks, and assess an organization's specific situation and recommend a course of action based on best practices that have worked well for other customers.

IBM offers a vast array of professional services for adopting SOA which fit into three broad categories:

- *Business professional services*—IBM Global Business Services (*http://www.ibm.com/services/soa/*) (GBS) offers consulting expertise to help businesses innovate using technology. Their engagement models help everyone from the CEO and CIO developing an SOA strategy for their enterprise to a line of business managers transforming their business to developers following the SOA lifecycle to develop applications.

- *Infrastructure professional services*—IBM Global Technology Services (GTS) offers consulting expertise to help businesses optimize their IT infrastructure targeting flexibility and return on investment (ROI). Their engagement models help everyone from CIOs evaluating their infrastructure's readiness for SOA to IT staffs designing and installing infrastructure management solutions.

- *Software professional services*—The IBM Software Group develops all of the products described earlier. IBM Software Services, part of the Software Group, offers consulting expertise targeted to help organizations leverage these and related products as the basis for SOA projects. They offer deep knowledge and skills transfer on how the products work and how to leverage them to successfully create business applications and operate them in production.

All three groups coordinate closely to leverage their particular expertise and drive customer value.

5
Development of an SOA Application

So far, we've looked at how to get started with SOA, the infrastructure needed to run SOA applications, and what products IBM offers to build that SOA infrastructure. Now let's take a brief look at how to develop SOA applications and how to govern their development.

SOA Lifecycle

SOA focuses on aligning IT with business, on modeling business as processes of reusable services, and on providing business with IT applications whose structure matches one-to-one with the structure of that business. Because every business is different, every business's SOA applications must be different from those for other, even similar businesses. This means that an enterprise, even one with reusable services at its disposal, must custom-develop the applications it needs that comprise the SOA that aligns with its business. This section discusses how to custom develop SOA applications.

Development of custom SOA applications makes use of the SOA lifecycle. The lifecycle controls the development of individual services, of applications, and even the coordination of developing multiple services and applications. Figure 5.1 illustrates the SOA lifecycle.

The lifecycle consists of five phases. These are discussed in detail below, but briefly, the phases are:

1. *Model*—Gather business requirements and design key business processes and develop the architecture.

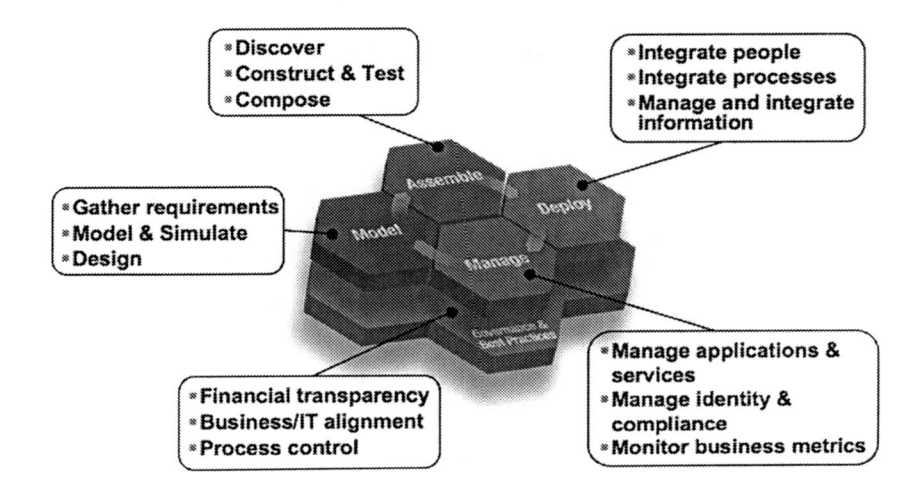

Figure 5.1. The SOA lifecycle.

2. *Assemble*—Integrate services and construct composite applications that implement the model.

3. *Deploy*—Put the composite applications and services into production.

4. *Manage*—Monitor and administer the applications and their environment.

5. *Govern*—Establish and ensure compliance with service lifecycle management processes.

The first thing to notice about the SOA lifecycle is that it's iterative. The first four phases—model, assemble, deploy, and manage—form a cycle that never ends. You can start at any point in the lifecycle—most common is to start with model or assemble. Governance is not a step in the lifecycle, but a way to control and manage all of the steps.

Secondly, the iterative SOA lifecycle fits well with incremental adoption of SOA. Earlier we discussed how an organization's conversion to SOA can be incremental or big bang, and how incremental adoption is lower risk and likely to be more successful. The lifecycle supports incremental adoption—running an iteration of the lifecycle for each increment. For example, one increment may develop a single ser-

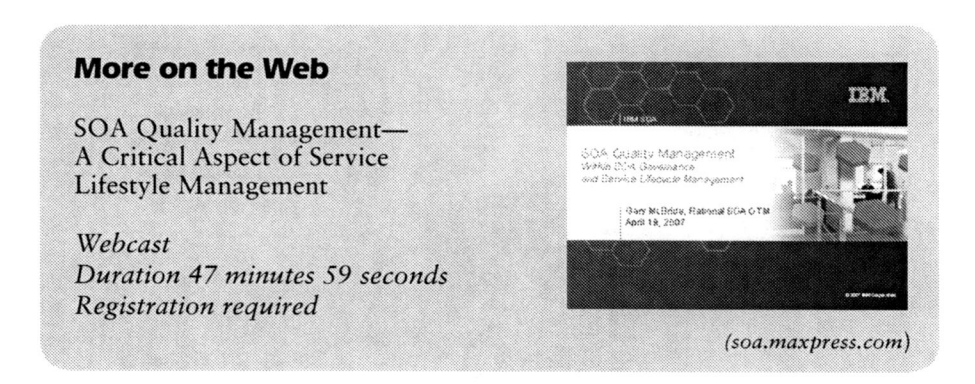

> **More on the Web**
>
> SOA Quality Management—
> A Critical Aspect of Service
> Lifestyle Management
>
> *Webcast*
> *Duration 47 minutes 59 seconds*
> *Registration required*
>
> (soa.maxpress.com)

vice, and then another increment may convert a small monolithic application into a composite application with several services. The lifecycle should be the process used to manage both increments.

Thirdly, the SOA lifecycle can be applied to any of the SOA entry points. A development team can use an entry point to discover the opportunity for a service, then can use the lifecycle as a process to develop the opportunity into a service, a functioning business asset used in production. Multiple teams can use the entry points to discover multiple opportunities and can independently follow the lifecycle to develop them into services, with governance coordinating these concurrent efforts.

SOA Lifecycle Phases

Given this overview of the SOA lifecycle, now let's look at the parts of the lifecycle in detail:

- *Model*—Gather business requirements and design key business processes. One very good way to begin an SOA iteration is by identifying key services and consumers. This is an opportunity to design, simulate, and optimize the business processes in consultation with the business experts to make sure they accurately model the way the business functions and perhaps even serve as a guide to improving business function. This is a very abstract model which can be produced easily and changed rapidly to facilitate understanding of the business and ensure a proper reflection of the business. This step is crucial to the success of the remainder of the lifecycle.

WebSphere Business Modeler is the main IBM product for the modeling step of the lifecycle.

- *Assemble*—Construct services and composite applications that implement the model. The model contains business processes and activities or other notions of needed services and how they'll be used. Now the development team searches for existing services in its catalog to fill these needs, and develops new services. New services may be implemented from scratch, by adapting existing legacy applications, by accessing partner services, and by combining existing services in new ways. Testing ensures that the new and previously existing services work as needed and fulfill the model as expected.

Rational Application Developer and WebSphere Integration Developer are the main IBM products for the assembly step of the lifecycle.

- *Deploy*—Put the composite applications into production. Once a composite application is assembled, it doesn't yet produce value until the users can use it. The enterprise needs an IT environment to deploy the application into one whose parts are well integrated and provide a secure, scalable, and high-throughput foundation for business applications. This environment and its applications integrate the people who use the applications with the processes they perform and the information they use, helping to ensure that all key parts of the enterprise are working together.

The main IBM products for the deployment step of the lifecycle are:

- WebSphere Process Server
- WebSphere Portal
- IBM Information Server
- WebSphere Enterprise Service Bus and WebSphere Message Broker
- WebSphere Adapters
- WebSphere Partner Gateway
- WebSphere Extended Deployment and WebSphere Datapower SOA Appliances

- *Manage*—Monitor and administer the applications and their environment. Ideally, an application can be deployed and then run forever error-free. In reality, errors occur in applications and environments fail. Applications and their environments must be monitored to confirm proper operation, to collect metrics, and to detect problems and provide notification. Applications and their environments must be administrated to correct problems and adjust configurations to optimize operations and avoid future problems. Monitoring and management should occur at both an IT level and a business level, letting both IT and business know how their respective domains are operating.

Tivoli Composite Application Manager for SOA is the main IBM product for the management step of the lifecycle.

- *Govern*—Control the lifecycle and coordinate independent users of the lifecycle. For an enterprise to use SOA effectively, it must focus its efforts where they will have the best payoff, must ensure that the services truly model the business as it ought to work, and must be sure that independent teams produce services that are reusable across teams and applications. This is a significant topic and is discussed in detail next.

WebSphere Service Registry and Repository is the main IBM product for the governance of the lifecycle.

SOA Governance

SOA governance is critical to the success of an organization's SOA efforts. Without it, teams and departments duplicate effort, may not share well, and may not have adequate funding for the value they're producing. SOA without governance can easily lead to service oriented chaos, which doesn't help the organization and hurts the reputation of SOA. We will see how to control the chaos by understanding governance, its challenges, its lifecycle, a process for performing the lifecycle, and products for governance.

In order to understand SOA governance, why it's important, and how to address it, we first need to understand: What is SOA governance? To do that, we need to understand governance and management in general, and then how SOA governance fits in.

Governance is the establishment of chains of responsibility to empower people, measurement to gauge effectiveness, policies to guide the organization to meet its goals, control mechanisms to ensure compliance, and communication to keep all required parties informed. Governance determines who is responsible for making decisions, what decisions need to be made, and policies for making decisions consistently.

Governance is different from management. Governance plans for what decisions will need to be made, whereas management is the process of making and implementing the decisions. Governance sets policies, whereas management follows them.

IT governance is, well, governance for IT—namely, the application of governance to an IT organization, its people, processes, and information to guide the way those assets support the needs of the business.

SOA governance is a specialization of IT governance that puts key IT governance decisions within the context of the lifecycle of service components, services, and business processes. It is the effective management of this lifecycle that is the key goal to SOA governance.

IT governance is broader than SOA governance. IT governance covers all aspects of IT, including issues that affect SOA like data models and security, as well as issues beyond SOA like data storage and desktop support. SOA governance addresses aspects of the service lifecycle such as planning, publishing, discovery, versioning, management, and security.

So back to the main question: Why is SOA governance important? SOA governance ensures that SOA accomplishes the desired business results. An SOA governance model focuses development efforts on the most valuable services and processes, makes sure that they're widely reusable, and ensures that they're being widely reused (and not reinvented). It facilitates communication between teams to help make their parts interoperable and reusable, and to help iron out agreements on functionality and quality of service. It prevents SOA from occurring in silos.

SOA governance aligns with IT governance and corporate governance, and if need be can help improve that alignment, as shown in Figure 5.2. Organizations with strong IT governance already focus on the alignment of IT with business; their adoption of SOA governance will focus primarily on SOA specifics, but in doing so will further strengthen the relationship between IT and business. Organizations whose IT governance historically has been somewhat weak can use SOA governance as a catalyst to improve their IT governance and strengthen the alignment between IT and business.

Another important question is: Who runs SOA governance? Governance should be performed by a group focused on that task; some examples of groups are an architectural review board, an executive steering committee, a business relationship director, or an SOA Center of Excellence. The governance group develops the governance model, implements it, communicates it to the rest of the enterprise,

More on the Web
- SOA Governance
- Service Oriented Chaos
- Desired Business Results

(soa.maxpress.com)

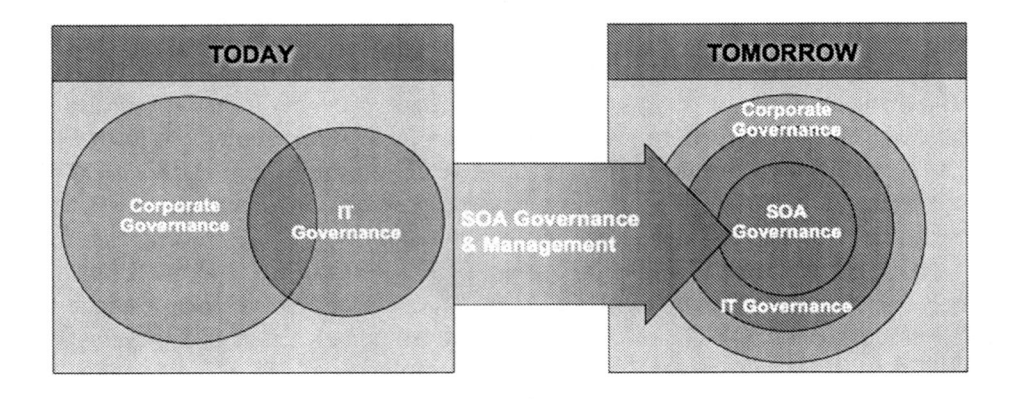

Figure 5.2. SOA governance aligns with IT and corporate governance.

ensures that it's being followed, and revises it as necessary. The group establishes policies for identification and development of services, establishment of service level agreements (SLAs), management of registries, and other efforts that provide effective governance. Group members then put those policies into practice, mentoring and assisting teams with developing services and composite applications.

SOA Governance Challenges

Everybody makes SOA sound so great. So, then: How can SOA lead to service oriented chaos?

SOA does not automatically make everything easier. In fact, SOA adds flexibility but complexity, which can make many IT practices more difficult. SOA governance is where the challenges of SOA become unavoidable and must be addressed. Here are some common SOA governance challenges that any SOA project must be prepared to tackle:

> **More on the Web**
>
> - SOA Governance
> - SOA Governance and the Prevention of Service Oriented Anarchy
> - A Case for SOA Governance
>
> *(soa.maxpress.com)*

- *Establishing decision rights*

- *Service ownership*—When multiple departments reuse a service and depend on it, then who is responsible for it? Someone has to be in charge of development, deployment, and maintenance.

- *Service funding*—Should one department fund the service when many departments benefit from it? How can the users of a service help fund it?

- *Defining appropriate services*

- *Service definition*—Services must be identified, scoped, and designed—all based on the needs of the business.

- *Service message model*—The service interface consists not only of operations, but also of request and reply messages whose formats need to be defined and agreed upon.

- *Service security*—Who is allowed to use a service, what are they allowed to do with the service, and does the data exchanged need to be protected?

- *Managing the lifecycle of service assets*

- *Service deployment lifecycle*—Once deployed, a service does not last forever. The deployment lifecycle for a service has five stages: planned, tested, active, deprecated, and sunsetted.

- *Service versioning*—Once a service is defined and deployed, its interface and functionality cannot be changed. Changes need to go into a new version, which can be an extension of the previous version and therefore backward compatible.

- *Service migration*—Service consumers need to be updated to use newer versions or newer services so that older ones can be sunsetted.

- *Service registries*—Enable providers to make their services known and consumers to use these services and to find the providers, both at design time and at runtime.

- *Measuring effectiveness*

- *Service testing*—Verifies that a provider does what it's supposed to do.

- *Service monitoring*—Supplies notification when providers stop working, before outages affect the applications and users.

Many of these challenges are not new. Creating and managing reusable assets always takes more work than for non-reusable ones. Meeting these challenges is an investment in making SOA successful.

SOA Governance Lifecycle

SOA without governance can become chaotic. So, then: How do we apply governance to SOA?

As we discussed earlier, SOA development follows a lifecycle. SOA governance also follows a corresponding lifecycle, as shown in Figure 5.3.

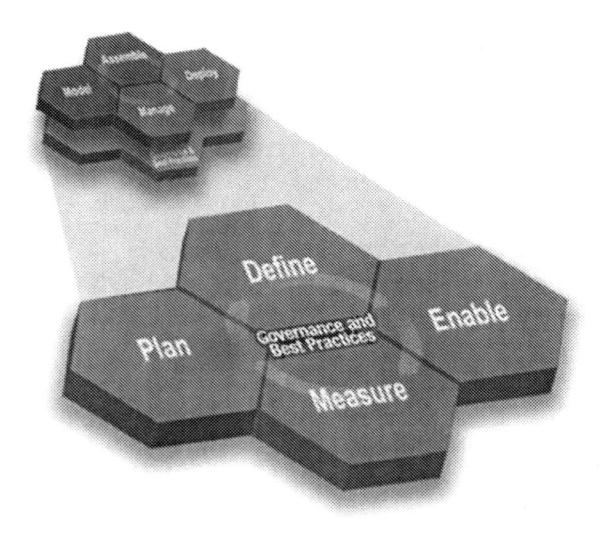

The SOA governance lifecycle defines four phases. Briefly, they are:

1. *Plan*—Establish the governance need. What are the immediate goals for the SOA initiative? What are the hurdles that the organization faces: cultural, technological, current corporate and IT governance practices? What can we reuse/extend in an IT governance model for SOA governance?

Figure 5.3. The SOA governance lifecycle.

2. *Define*—Design the governance approach. What are the integration standards? The organizational structures? How will change management be performed? How will services be identified, approved for development, and funded? How will the organization know if it's being successful?

> **More on the Web**
> - Advancing SOA Goverance and Service Lifestyle Management
> - IBM SOA Governance Lifecycle
> - SOA Goverance and Service Management
>
> *(soa.maxpress.com)*

3. *Enable*—Put the governance model into action. Now that the governance processes and policies have been defined, start doing them.

4. *Measure*—Monitor and manage the governance processes. This makes sure that SOA is working as envisioned and that governance is being effective.

The governance lifecycle produces a governance model which is used to manage the SOA lifecycle. Simply put, a governance model "describes what is supposed to be done, how it is supposed to be done, and who is responsible for doing what" (Eichhorst). The model is expressed as artifacts such as processes, organization, and tooling. These artifacts guide the management of the SOA lifecycle, helping the enterprise conform to best practices and maximize effectiveness.

SOA Governance and Management Method

SOA governance has a lifecycle that goes with the SOA lifecycle. So, then: How do we apply the SOA governance lifecycle to the SOA lifecycle?

The IBM SOA Governance and Management Method (SGMM) is a full process for performing the SOA governance lifecycle so that governance can be applied to the SOA lifecycle. The lifecycle and method phases are the same, but the method expands greatly on what tasks to perform in each phase.

Let's look at the method phases in detail:

- *Plan*—Determine the governance focus. Assess the need for governance and determine what the governance efforts need to focus on for that iteration of governance work. Typical tasks include:

- Perform a tailoring workshop to customize the method for the iteration goals and the existing governance environment.

- Assess the existing governance mechanisms so the iteration will extend, not replace, existing governance structures.

- Define the scope of governance: business governance, development governance, service management governance, or all of these?

- Conduct a change-readiness survey to determine how much extension will be possible.

- *Define*—Define the SOA governance model. There are several aspects of SOA governance to be defined: an ownership and funding model, a board to manage the policies established by governance, the processes to be governed, the identification and development of services, roles and responsibilities, quality metrics, tooling, and planning. Steps performed in this stage include:

  - Define and refine the governance processes.

  - Define the organizational change that will be produced.

  - Define the IT changes in SOA development.

- *Enable*—Implement the SOA governance model. Tasks include:

  - Implement the transition plan.

  - Initiate the SOA organizational changes.

  - Launch the SOA center of excellence.

  - Implement the infrastructure for SOA.

- *Measure*—Refine the SOA governance model. Use the metrics defined to determine whether governance is being followed and is achieving the desired effects. This means performing tasks like:

  - Measure the effectiveness of the governance processes.

  - Measure the effectiveness of the organizational change.

  - Review and refine the operational environment.

SGMM is performed iteratively to impose governance gradually and refine it as an organization becomes more comfortable with SOA. Each of the iterations tries to preserve the existing governance mechanisms from previous iterations by extending them. The method is flexible and can be tailored at the beginning of each iteration for the specific needs of the organization.

> **More on the Web**
>
> - IBM SOA Governance and Management Method
> - Rational Method Composer Plug-in for SOA Goverance
> - IBM SOA/Web Services Center of Excellence
>
> *(soa.maxpress.com)*

SOA Governance Products

Most products for architecting, developing, and managing SOA applications and infrastructure have a governance aspect to them as well. IBM's products for SOA are discussed earlier. One that deserves particular attention is WebSphere Service Registry and Repository. This product is used to implement a service registry, which is a key point for enforcement of governance decisions, simply by making a service and particular providers either available or unavailable.

A product to help perform the SOA governance lifecycle in general and SGMM specifically is the SOA Governance plug-in for IBM Rational Method Composer. IBM Global Business Services (GBS) offers consulting engagements for establishing SOA governance such as the IBM SOA/Web Services Center of Excellence offering.

6

Conclusion: Building an SOA Application

In this overview of IBM SOA technology, we've touched upon several aspects of what an organization needs to do to successfully adopt SOA:

- How to get started with SOA

- Methodologies for discovering and developing services

- Visualizing the capabilities of an SOA application infrastructure using the SOA reference architecture

- Creating an SOA application infrastructure using IBM products

- Developing SOA applications using the SOA lifecycle, SOA programming model, and SOA governance lifecycle.

Although each aspect has a lot of details, one overarching theme not to be missed is how well these aspects all fit together. As Figure 6.1 shows, the entry points discover services that can be developed using the SOA lifecycle, which is managed by SOA governance. The service providers can be implemented as service components using service component architecture (SCA), a programming model specifically for SOA, which can be deployed into WebSphere Process Server. In turn, WebSphere Process Server—along with WebSphere Enterprise Service Bus and WebSphere In-

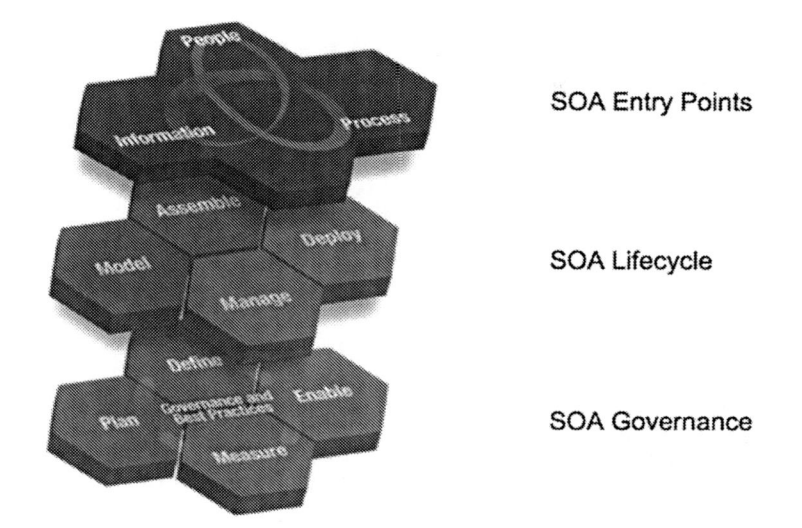

Figure 6.1. Building out IBM's SOA capabilities.

tegration Developer—implements many of the capabilities of the SOA reference architecture, and IBM has other products for other capabilities which an organization can add to its installation of the reference architecture as it discovers the need for those capabilities.

About the Author

Bobby Woolf

Bobby Woolf earns a living as a member of IBM Software Services for WebSphere, consultants who help customers achieve success with WebSphere products, where he assists clients in developing applications with service oriented architecture. He is an IBM Certified SOA Solution Designer, a co-author of *Enterprise Integration Patterns* and *The Design Patterns Smalltalk Companion* (both from Addison-Wesley), has published numerous articles and podcasts at IBM developerWorks and elsewhere, and frequently presents at conferences. He also authors a very popular blog, "WebSphere SOA and J2EE in Practice."

Index

A
access services, 30–31
access to existing applications, products, 41
adapters, WebSphere Application Adapters, 41
adopting
    new technology, 9–10
    SOA, 1–9, 54–55
appliances. *See* WebSphere Datapower SOA Appliances
applications, defined, 26–27
architecture
    current, 7
    See also reference architecture
assembling, SOA lifecycle phase, 59

B
benefits. *See* value
business application services
    defined, 30
    products, 41
business dashboards, 34–35
business goals, 4–5
business modeling, 34
business monitoring, 34
business object maps, 51
business process, 53
Business Process Choreographer (BPC), 53
Business Process Execution Language (BPEL), 53
business process management, products, 39–40
business professional services, 54–55
business rules, 54
business services
    defined, 34
    products, 45–46
business state machines, 53

C
Centers of Excellence (COE), 12–13
challenges
    governance, 62–64
    overview, 8
choreography, service, 53
clustering, WebSphere Application Server Network Deployment, 47
Component Business Modeling (CBM), 15
components, defined, 26
composite applications, defined, 26–27
connectivity entry point, 23–25
constraints, 5–8
core, 49–51

D
dashboards, business, 34–35
define, governance phase, 66
deploying, SOA lifecycle phase, 59
development, 56–67
    governance, 60–67
    lifecycle, 56–60
    products, 43
development services, 33
distribution, ESB, 32
dynamic service selection, 52

E
enable, governance phase, 66
entry points, 16–25
    defined, 14

methodology, 16–18
evolution, integration approaches, 3

F
flows. *See* mediation flows

G
goals, business, 4–5
govern, SOA lifecycle phase, 60
governance
    development, 60–67
    methodology, 15

H
human interaction, products, 39
human tasks, BEPL, 53

I
information entry point, 20–22
information services
    defined, 30
    products, 40
infrastructure services, 32–33
integration, ESB, 31
interaction services
    defined, 29
    products, 39
interface maps, 51

L
lifecycle
    governance, 64–65
    SOA development, 56–60

M
management
    method and governance, 65–67
    products, 43–45
    services, 33–34
    SOA lifecycle phase, 59–60
    versus governance, 61
maps, SOA core, 51
measure, governance phase, 66
mediation, ESB, 31–32
mediation flows, 51

methodologies, 14–25
    entry points, 16–25
    overview, 14–15
modeling
    business, 34
    SOA lifecycle phase, 58
monitoring, business, 34

O
operational readiness, 7
organizational readiness, 6–7

P
partner services
    defined, 30
    products, 40
people entry point, 18–19
phases
    governance, 65–67
    SOA lifecycle, 58–60
plan, governance phase, 65–66
process entry point, 19–20
Process Server Component Model, 48–54
process server embedded products, 46–48
process services, 29
products, 36–48
    deployment phase, 59
    governance, 67
    process server embedded, 46–48
    reference architecture, 36–41
    service connectivity, 41–46
professional services, SOA adoption, 54–55
projects, 10–15

R
Rational Application Developer for WebSphere Software, 43
Rational Software Architect, 43
readiness
    operational, 7
    organizational, 6–7
reference architecture
    about, 28–29
    products, 36–41
registry. *See* service registry

relationships, SOA core, 51–52
reuse entry point, 22–23
rules. *See* business rules

S
servers
    Process Server Component Model, 48–54
    process server embedded products, 46–48
    WebSphere Application Server, 44
    WebSphere Application Server Network Deployment, 47–48
    WebSphere Process Server, 39–40, 47, 48
    WebSphere Process Server Component Model, 46–55
service bus, 31
service choreography, 53
Service Component Architecture (SCA), 50
service connectivity, 23–25
    about, 31–32
    products, 41–46
service consumers, connecting to, 27
service coordinator, 27
Service Data Objects (SDO), 50
Service Integration Maturity Model (SIMM), 14
service management, products, 44
Service Oriented Modeling Architecture (SOMA), 14–15
service providers, 27, 29–31
service registry, 32
service security, products, 44–45
service support, 32–35
SOA Governance and Management Method (SGMM), 15
standards
    SOA application infrastructure, 35
    SOA core, 50

state machines, business, 53

T
terminology, 26–27
Tivoli Access Manager for e-business, 45
Tivoli Change and Configuration Management Database, 45
Tivoli Dynamic Workload Broker, 38
Tivoli Federated Identity Manager, 44–45

V
value
    connectivity entry point, 23–25
    entry points, 18
    governance, 61
    information entry point, 20–22
    people entry point, 18–19
    process entry point, 19–20
    reuse entry point, 22–23

W
WebSphere Application Adapters, 41
WebSphere Application Server, 44
WebSphere Application Server Network Deployment, 47–48
WebSphere Business Monitor, 46
WebSphere Business Services Fabric, 46
WebSphere Datapower SOA Appliances, 38–39
WebSphere Enterprise Service Bus, 42, 48
WebSphere Extended Deployment, 37–38
WebSphere Integration Developer, 43
WebSphere Message Broker, 42
WebSphere Partner Gateway, 40
WebSphere Portal, 39
WebSphere Process Server, 39–40, 47, 48
WebSphere Process Server Component Model, 46–55
WebSphere Service Registry and Repository, 42

Reader Feedback Sheet

Your comments and suggestions are very important in shaping future publications. Please e-mail us at *info@maxpress.com* or photocopy this page, jot down your thoughts, and fax it to (850) 934-9981 or mail it to:

Maximum Press
Attn: Jim Hoskins
605 Silverthorn Road
Gulf Breeze, FL 32561

_____
_____
_____
_____
_____
_____
_____
_____
_____
_____
_____
_____
_____

*Exploring IBM SOA
Technology & Practice*
by Bobby Woolf
161 pages
ebook
$44.95
ISBN: 978-0-9773569-2-8

*IBM On Demand
Technology Made Simple
Third Edition*
by Jim Hoskins
96 pages
$29.95
ISBN: 0-9773569-1-4

*Understanding IBM Workplace
Strategy & Products,
Second Edition*
by Ron Sebastian &
Douglas W. Spencer
184 pages
$39.95
ISBN: 1-931644-45-4

*Protect Your Great Ideas
for Free!*
J. Nevin Shaffer, Jr., Esq.
184 pages
$29.95
ISBN: 1-931644-47-0

*101 Ways to Promote
Your Web Site, Sixth Edition*
by Susan Sweeney, C.A.
432 pages
$29.95
ISBN: 1-931644-46-2

*101 Internet Businesses You
Can Start From Home,
Second Edition*
by Susan Sweeney, C.A.
336 pages
$29.95
ISBN: 1-931644-48-9

*3G Marketing on the Internet,
Seventh Edition*
by Susan Sweeney, C.A., Andy
MacLellen & Ed Dorey
216 pages
$34.95
ISBN: 1-931644-37-3

Podcasting for Profit
Leesa Barnes
376 pages
$34.95
ISBN: 978-1-931644-57-0

To purchase a Maximum Press book, visit your local bookstore
or call 1-850-934-4583. Online ordering available at *www.maxpress.com*